Winning With Diversity

A Practical Handbook for Creating Inclusive Meetings, Events, and Organizations

by Donald M. Norris and M.C. Joëlle Fignolé Lofton

American Society of Association Executives Foundation
International Association for Exposition Management Foundation
International Association of Convention and Visitor Bureaus Foundation
Meeting Professionals International Foundation
Professional Convention Management Association Education Foundation

Library of Congress Cataloging-in-Publication Data

Norris, Donald M.
    Winning with diversity : a practical handbook for creating
  inclusive meetings, events, and organizations / by Donald M. Norris
  and M.C. Jooëlle Fignolé Lofton.
        p.   cm.
    Includes bibliographical references.
    ISBN 0-88034-093-2
    1. Diversity in the workplace. 2. Communication in organizations.
· 3. Intercultural communication. 4. Diversity in the workplace--Case
  studies.   I. Lofton, M. C. Joëlle Fignolé (Marie Camille Joëlle
  Fignolé), 1958-   . II. Title.
  HF5549.5.M5N67   1994
  658.3'1244--dc20   94-43566
                                                           CIP

Edited by Sandra Sabo
Cover design by Dyer Design
Interior design by Dahlman-Middour Design

Copyright © 1995 by the American Society of Association Executives
Foundation, International Association for Exposition Management Foundation,
International Association of Convention & Visitor Bureaus Foundation, Meeting
Professionals International Foundation, and Professional Convention
Management Association Education Foundation

ISBN 0-88048-093-2

Printed in the United States of America

TABLE OF CONTENTS

ACKNOWLEDGMENTS

Five organizations conceived and sponsored this project to create a book and supporting materials that would make meeting planners, association executives, and other professionals in the hospitality industry more aware of the importance of building inclusive work environments. The coalition included the Foundations of the American Society of Association Executives, the International Association of Convention and Visitor Bureaus, International Association for Exposition Management, Meeting Professionals International, and the Professional Convention Management Association.

This book addresses the particular needs of professionals involved in meeting and event management, the hospitality industry, and association management. (Figure 1 shows the primary and secondary audiences specifically targeted by this book.) The examples and techniques discussed, however, apply to any enterprise grappling with the challenges of diversity in the 21st century marketplace.

Together, the five sponsoring organizations have approximately 50,000 members who, in turn, serve millions of employees, members, and customers. If all these organizations and their constituencies commit to winning with diversity in their marketplaces, they will dramatically affect American society.

FIGURE 1 - AUDIENCES AMONG SPONSORING ORGANIZATIONS

	ASAE	IACVB	IAEM	MPI	PCMA
Member Audience	• Association Executives	• Convention and Visitor Bureaus (CVBs)	• Exposition Managers • International Fair Organizers • Staff with Meeting/ Exposition Responsibility	• Corporate & Association Meeting Managers • Independent Meeting Managers • Medical Meeting Managers	• Association Meeting Planners
Associate/Secondary Audience	• Associate Members –Hotels –Meeting Planning Consultants –Other Consultants –Suppliers • Insurance • Printing • Travel • Technology • Volunteer Leaders of Member Organizations	• Suppliers: Any Business in the Community • Meeting Professionals –Corporate –Association • Tour Operators • Travel/ Tourism Representatives	• Suppliers to the Industry –Hotels –Airlines –Exhibits –Audio Visual –Printing –Destination Marketing –CVBs –Speakers Bureaus –Technology –Travel –Other Suppliers –Service Contractors	• Suppliers to the Industry –Hotels –Airlines –Exhibits –Audio Visual –Printing –Destination Marketing –CVBs –Speakers Bureaus –Technology –Travel –Other Suppliers	• Suppliers to the Industry –Hotels –Airlines –Exhibits –Audio Visual –Printing –Destination Marketing –CVBs –Speakers Bureaus –Other Suppliers

ASAE   American Society of Association Executives

IACVB   International Association of Convention and Visitor Bureaus

IAEM   International Association for Exposition Management

MPI   Meeting Professionals International

PCMA   Professional Convention Management Association

FOREWORD

In March 1993 volunteer leaders and staff of several leading industry organizations met to address an issue that concerned us all: diversity. An historic agreement was reached to tackle this broad and important subject and a Unity Team was organized with representatives from the Foundations of the American Society of Association Executives, International Association of Convention & Visitor Bureaus, International Association for Exposition Management, Meeting Professionals International and the Professional Convention Management Association. The result is this book, a tribute to the cooperative spirit and energy of a host of volunteers and staff from the five organizations involved.

The unique concept of bringing together the ASAE, IACVB, IAEM, MPI and PCMA Foundations could not have materialized without the leadership and support of R. William Taylor, CAE, President, ASAE; Stephen C. Carey, CAE, Executive Director, IACVB; Steven G. Hacker, CAE, President, IAEM; Edwin L. Griffin, Jr., CAE, Executive Vice President/CEO, MPI; and Roy B. Evans, Jr., CAE, Executive Vice President/CEO, PCMA.

Winning With Diversity is the result of a search for best practice within a broad spectrum of organizations both inside and outside the association, hospitality, and meetings industries. Authors Norris and Fignolé Lofton, along with their research team at Strategic Initiatives, interviewed more than 50 organizations on the forefront of the diversity issue. You will learn how "doing the right thing" can also make good business sense, as example after example illustrates how building an inclusive organization can increase productivity, help you better serve your marketplace, and give your organization the competitive edge.

I would like especially to acknowledge the leadership role of the Unity Team which guided this project from its beginnings in 1993 to completion: Garis F. Distelhorst, CAE, National Association of College Stores, Chairman, ASAE Foundation; Marian L. Holt, San Jose Convention & Visitors Bureau, Chair, IACVB Foundation; Steven G. Hacker, CAE, International Association for Exposition Management and President, IAEM Foundation; and John L. Fuller, Jr., ITT Sheraton Corporation, Chairman, MPI Foundation.

A special thanks to Ann C. Kenworthy, CAE, Executive Director, ASAE Foundation, who kept us moving down the right path.

We are also greatly indebted to the Joint Diversity Project Task Force, a group of professionals in all segments of the industry who lent their time, insight, and expertise to the research team throughout the process. Their support and knowledge were invaluable.

Those of us on the Unity Team hope you will find practical solutions to the challenges you face, as well as renewed enthusiasm for building a truly inclusive organization. We wish you great success in leading your organization to even higher performance through diversity.

We look forward to the Unity Team carrying on with projects that will have a universal benefit to our industry.

David R. Evans
Vice President & General Sales Manager, Westin Hotels & Resorts
Chairman, Unity Team/Chairman, PCMA Foundation

ABOUT THE AUTHORS

D r. Donald M. Norris is President of Strategic Initiatives, Inc., a management consulting firm in Herndon, Virginia. Dr. Norris has worked as a consultant, author, researcher, and university administrator for over 20 years. He is a nationally known author and practitioner in the fields of strategic planning, strategic marketing, and the use of information technology as a tool of transformation. He and Ms. Fignolé Lofton have collaborated on three books for the association community: *Market Driven Management: Lessons Learned From 20 Successful Associations, Getting Your Association Hooked on Quality—A How-to Guide for CEOs, Volunteers, and Staff*, and now, *Winning With Diversity*. He has also written several works under the sponsorship of the Society for College and University Planning: *A Guide for New Planners* and *Transforming Higher Education: A Learning Vision for the 21st Century* (forthcoming).

Ms. M.C. Joelle Fignolé Lofton is President of Elements in Style, Inc., a publications development firm in North Potomac, Maryland. While specializing in helping firms solve publications problems and tailor their communications, she works enthusiastically as an author, facilitator, and guest speaker. For more than ten years, Ms. Fignolé Lofton has developed documents, primarily in the health/medical and postsecondary education arenas. She has served as a researcher and consultant for Federal agencies, consulting firms, and university departments by translating technical jargon into readable prose for lay audiences, distilling research papers into useable formats for policy makers and specialists, and presenting information gleaned from interviews and literature searches. Ms. Fignolé Lofton has participated in numerous projects with Strategic Initiatives.

Strategic Initiatives, Inc., specializes in developing organizational strategies for the 21st century—the Age of Information. Using a core of senior consultants and a network of affiliated associates as a pool, Dr. Norris assembles consulting teams aligned with the precise needs of clients. These strategic teams help clients develop the visions, strategies, and programs to transform themselves into high-performing, 21st century organizations. This requires the crafting of initiatives dealing with diversity and inclusiveness, organizational development, information technology, customer service, empowerment, total quality management and continuous quality improvement, and market driven management. Strategic Initiatives' clients range from major corporations and emerging high-tech businesses, to colleges and universities, to associations and other nonprofits.

WHY DIVERSITY? WHY INCLUSIVENESS?

N
o person and no organization doing business in the 1990s can afford to ignore diversity.

Suppose, for example, you're a meeting professional called in by an association whose last annual meeting drew nothing but complaints from minority attendees. They had found the service personnel surly and patronizing, the music old-fashioned, and the program uninviting and impenetrable to newcomers. This experience has jeopardized the association's genuine efforts to attract minority members, and you're asked to suggest remedial actions. *How can you help the association understand and overcome these problems?*

Maybe your corporation plans to hold a meeting for key staff and sales reps from all over the country. The CEO asks you, the corporate meeting professional, to reevaluate the program schedule, recreational activities, use of alcohol, menus, suggested attire, and type of room set-ups. In doing so, you're asked to consider the increasing number of women in the sales force and employees' increased health consciousness. Also, the CEO wants to make greater use of technology to facilitate preparation for the session. You'll need to encourage older staff to overcome their reticence and embrace these new technologies. *Where do you begin?*

Or perhaps you're the consultant to a large trade association that has failed to achieve its goals for a new set of programs. The board of directors asks you to determine what caused the initiatives to fail. Your analysis shows that although focus groups were used to explore market potential, the groups didn't represent the diversity of the target market. Moreover, the product development team, association leaders, and board members are almost all white men. *How can you tell the board that you've found the problem—and the board is part of it?*

Here are some additional scenarios to consider:
- As director of communications for a regional trade association, you and your staff have worked hard to make your publications sensitive to a diverse readership. You've eliminated characterizations and references that would offend women and minorities and always portrayed the diversity of your membership in pictures and print. But your efforts seem stuck in low gear. The executive director has asked you to develop a plan for using communications to aggressively portray your association's commitment to diversity. *How can you meet this request?*
- A hotel corporation has just hired you to manage its marketing division. The staff is in disarray, acting as individuals rather than as a team.

Not only is intolerance rampant, but also some staff have accused their colleagues of racism and sexism. Not surprisingly, commitment and productivity are low. *Where and how do you start corrective action?*

- You're a white male executive who perceives the need to develop your skills to deal more effectively with women, racial and ethnic minorities, and international meeting participants. You also want to increase the diversity of the teams that make major decisions for your organization. Yet you feel uncomfortable with earlier diversity initiatives. *What should you do?*

Welcome to the 1990s! If you haven't already faced similar situations and raised similar questions, it's only a matter of time. If you want to win with diversity and create high-performing organizations, this book is for you.

WHY THIS BOOK IS DIFFERENT

Diversity is one of the most talked about issues in America today. Hundreds of books and articles have been written on the subject; scores of seminars, workshops, and conferences focus on diversity every year; and legions of consultants are helping organizations to value and capitalize on the diversity of their workforce.

This book isn't about theories. It's based on the efforts of real organizations intent on using diversity to achieve success in their marketplace. Specifically, our goal is to demonstrate how professionals in the hospitality, meeting planning, and association industries—and the companies that serve them—can use diversity in their favor.

By effectively serving diverse customers, employing sensitivity when planning meetings, and creating communications for multifaceted readerships, the organizations profiled on the following pages build inclusiveness. They also earn a commitment to shared values from a diverse and motivated workforce, which enhances productivity and establishes competitive advantage. In these organizational contexts, "doing the right thing" also makes good business sense. In other words, there's a bottom-line argument in favor of diversity and inclusiveness. That marketplace argument can overcome any resistance to diversity.

Based on best-practice examples, this book will help you move beyond merely valuing diversity to building an inclusive, high-performing organization. In the process, diversity ceases to be merely a human resource initiative and becomes a fundamental competency: Diversity and inclusiveness become the responsibility of everyone in the organization.

WHY DIVERSITY IS FOR EVERYONE

You'll hear many perspectives on the notion of diversity. Some people believe that only white males should be concerned about diversity because "they're the ones who have to change." Essentially, white males become the target.

Others feel that a particular minority, ethnic, or gender group—or a cross-section of these groups— "own" diversity. In other words, members of these groups have the special role of explaining and interpreting their experiences to the majority. In this view, these groups always had to understand the majority culture; now the majority culture must understand and value them. Still others believe that diversity means replacing older white males in particular positions with a new majority coalition of women and people of different racial and ethnic groups.

As their basis, these perspectives rely on a concept of individual and group empowerment. Such views characterize the first stage of evolution from a single dominant culture. Furthermore, they are valid and even valuable at certain times. But the experiences of the organizations we studied suggest that these ideas fall short of achieving inclusiveness. Instead, their success stories recommend a model that makes diversity everyone's concern and spreads responsibility for behavior that affirms inclusiveness.

Key Definitions

To understand why diversity is for everyone, we need to establish the definition and evolution of six key concepts (see Chapter 1 for a more detailed explanation):

1. Diversity means difference. In its earliest definition, valuing diversity meant understanding and valuing the characteristics and capabilities of a narrowly defined set of targeted racial, ethnic, and gender groups— blacks, Hispanics, Native Americans, Asian Americans/Pacific Islanders, and women. Diversity simply meant people in these groups.

Over time, however, the definition of diversity expanded to include a wider range of ethnic and racial characteristics, including age, physical abilities, family status, lifestyle preferences, socioeconomic status, religious and spiritual values, language, and geographic location. Organizations have tried to create work environments that are friendly to the full range of people displaying these characteristics. White males have been included among the groups requiring consideration as components of diversity and treated as part of the solution, not as the problem.

In addition to adding new characteristics to the concept of diversity, we've come to understand that any particular group will exhibit a tremendous range in values and characteristics. One size does not fit all: Group stereotypes have no place in the 1990s organization.

Under this more sophisticated definition, diversity includes every employee, member, and customer. Each must be afforded the respect of being treated as someone whose wants and needs will be understood and addressed. Everyone in the organization must develop the awareness necessary to achieve this level of understanding. In today's diverse organization, *every* person has a great deal to learn.

Exhibit 1 - The Evolution of the Concept of Diversity

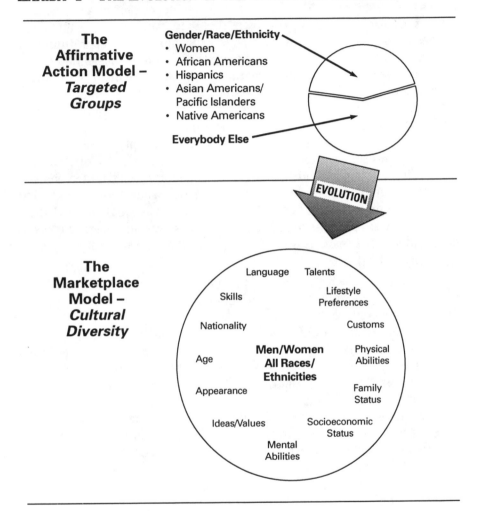

The Affirmative Action Model – *Targeted Groups*

Gender/Race/Ethnicity
- Women
- African Americans
- Hispanics
- Asian Americans/ Pacific Islanders
- Native Americans

Everybody Else

EVOLUTION

The Marketplace Model – *Cultural Diversity*

Language Talents

Skills Lifestyle Preferences

Nationality Customs

Men/Women All Races/ Ethnicities

Age Physical Abilities

Appearance Family Status

Ideas/Values Socioeconomic Status

Mental Abilities

This broadening of the concept of diversity characterizes the move from an affirmative action model to a marketplace model. Exhibit 1 illustrates this evolution.

2. Organizational Culture refers to the particular set of policies, practices, values, and expectations that define a workplace and guide the treatment of members or customers. The founders of most organizations developed the culture, with successive waves of management making modifications. These managers—typically middle-aged white males with homemaker wives—designed both formal and informal structures as if every worker were just like them. Or perhaps they developed the culture based on outmoded, stereotypical expectations of the capacities of minorities and women. These expectations lived on, buried in organizational culture, long after the stereotypes had been discredited.

Monocultural and exclusive organizational cultures like these impede the performance of a diverse workforce. They must be changed.

3. Barriers to Performance represent those hidden obstacles that exist in exclusive organizations. These are often unintentional and unrecognized by leadership—but they're real. To win commitment from a diverse workforce, organizations must identify and eliminate these barriers. They must make "enablers of high performance" available to everyone.

Not all barriers to performance have equal importance or prove easy to correct. For example, barriers based on residual racial prejudice and gender stereotypes are especially pernicious. Organizations that are winning with diversity have found that first dealing with inadvertent yet easily corrected barriers helps tackle the more intractable barriers.

4. Multiculturalism refers to a condition in which the organization represents, values, understands, and respects several distinct cultures. The classic multicultural situation exists in many international settings, where distinctive ethnic or cultural groups must understand and respect one another if they are to do business together and succeed.

5. Pluralism refers to a condition in which members of diverse ethnic, racial, religious, or social groups maintain their traditional cultures or special interests within a common (shared) culture. Pluralistic organizations recognize and value diversity, and they aggressively eliminate barriers to performance that fall unevenly on particular groups.

6. Inclusiveness is the act of encouraging belonging. Leaders of an inclusive organization do more than value diversity—they understand and aggressively eliminate barriers to performance that fall unevenly on different groups. In addition to creating a pluralistic culture, they establish standards of behavior that affirm inclusiveness. These leaders expect *all* employees to meet the standards.

Inclusive organizations motivate employees and generate intensive commitment, while at the same time meeting world-class performance standards. They use diverse teams to solve complex problems that involve highly diverse customer populations. The inclusive organization becomes a high-performing organization when it achieves these standards of performance.

Overview of the Contents

This handbook is grounded in the experiences of real enterprises that are winning with diversity. Our search for success stories led us to screen more than 100 organizations, of which we ultimately talked to representatives of more than 50. The interviewees spanned a wide range of settings and responsibilities, including corporate leaders from the hospitality industry; meeting professionals from international, corporate, and association settings; human resource managers in corporations and associations; association leaders; academic leaders; and specialists in student recruitment and retention.

In all of the organizations we found a growing interest in the subject of diversity. We also detected increasing levels of sophistication; many had experienced only the first wave of diversity programs and were just moving into the managing diversity stage. Others were more advanced and already grappling with managing diversity. A few had moved into the phase of going beyond a diversity-driven model to build a high-performing, inclusive organization. All were convinced that dealing effectively with diversity contributed positively to their current level of performance. Diversity, they said, would be absolutely critical to their long-term success. (See Appendix A for a more detailed explanation of the stages of diversity development.)

We've organized this book so you can scan some sections and jump to the topics of greatest interest. The first chapter, "Using Diversity to Build Inclusive Organizations," presents our basic model of building the capacity to win with diversity. Chapters 2 through 9 present eight types of changes in the behavior of organizations and individuals. Each begins with one or more brief case studies that discuss how exemplary organizations have dealt with various aspects of diversity. These chapters also present "Practical Applications" in the forms of "Lessons Learned" and "Helpful Hints" to guide you in applying the findings to your work environment. Each concludes with brief vignettes that describe the diversity-based activities of corporations, associations, or nonprofit organizations.

Chapter 10 poses and answers pointed questions, such as "What is the role of white men in diversity?" and "How can we avoid diversity backlash?" The last chapter, "Helping Your Organization Win With Diversity," provides analytic tools you can use to assess your organization's readiness for inclusiveness and to develop an action plan.

Appendix B, an annotated bibliography, lists recommended materials for a diversity library. In Appendix C you'll find information on the project's participants and the names of people who provided information for the vignettes.

How to Use This Book

Everyone confronting the challenges and opportunities presented by a diverse workforce and marketplace will find this book useful. Still, busy readers must cut to the chase. Exhibit 2 summarizes how you might approach this book if you're a meeting professional, board member, human resource professional, marketing manager, communications director, membership director, or other line manager.

As you read about what other organizations are doing—and consider what your organization might do—keep in mind that diversity is for and about everyone. Good luck.

Donald Norris   Herndon, Virginia
M.C. Joëlle Fignolé Lofton   December 1994

Exhibit 2 - How To Use This Book

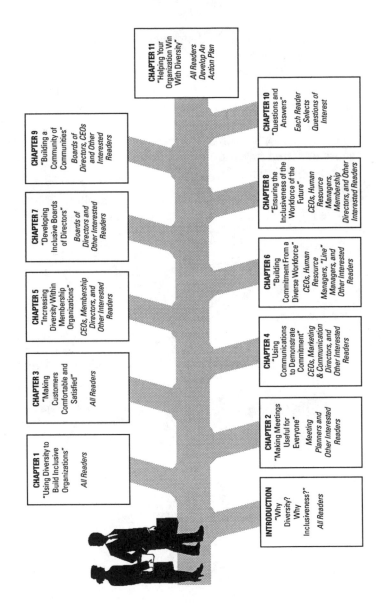

CHAPTER 11
"Helping Your Organization Win With Diversity"

All Readers Develop An Action Plan

CHAPTER 9
"Building a Community of Communities"

Boards of Directors, CEOs and Other Interested Readers

CHAPTER 10
"Questions and Answers"

Each Reader Selects Questions of Interest

CHAPTER 7
"Developing Inclusive Boards of Directors"

Boards of Directors and Other Interested Readers

CHAPTER 8
"Ensuring the Inclusiveness of the Workforce of the Future"

CEOs, Human Resource Managers, Membership Directors, and Other Interested Readers

CHAPTER 5
"Increasing Diversity Within Membership Organizations"

CEOs, Membership Directors, and Other Interested Readers

CHAPTER 6
"Building Commitment From a Diverse Workforce"

CEOs, Human Resource Managers, "Line" Managers, and Other Interested Readers

CHAPTER 3
"Making Customers Comfortable and Satisfied"

All Readers

CHAPTER 4
"Using Communications to Demonstrate Commitment"

CEOs, Marketing & Communication Directors, and Other Interested Readers

CHAPTER 1
"Using Diversity to Build Inclusive Organizations"

All Readers

CHAPTER 2
"Making Meetings Useful for Everyone"

Meeting Planners and Other Interested Readers

INTRODUCTION
"Why Diversity? Why Inclusiveness?"

All Readers

USING DIVERSITY TO BUILD INCLUSIVE ORGANIZATIONS

Diversity is for everyone, not just white male managers or members of targeted groups. It's a fundamental issue for every person in your community and for every person in your organization, from the board of directors to top management to the front-line workers who come face-to-face with customers. So how can your organization use diversity not to focus on differences but to build inclusiveness around a shared set of values?

This is a daunting question, considering that differences among people in the United States seem to overwhelm the values and goals that bind them together. Corporations, community groups, philanthropic organizations, and trade and professional associations face the challenge of creating an oasis of commitment in the desert of an imperfect world.

A DEFINING ISSUE FOR THE UNITED STATES

As the population of the United States continues to diversify, organizations in both the public and private sectors struggle to understand and serve their clients, customers, and stakeholders—who continually clamor for new products, new services, and improved performance. These constituencies also demand to be understood, individually and in groups, in terms of race, ethnicity, gender, age, nationality, education, religion, sexual orientation, class, family condition, geography, and a host of other characteristics.

Arguably, the United States has more experience than other nations in accepting significant immigrant populations, tolerating religious and cultural differences, and transforming its social values and national identity in the face of new realities and new citizens. To be sure, America's course has often been erratic and sometimes tumultuous. The legacy of racism continues to haunt the country, which hasn't yet fulfilled the promise of its enduring ideals. But Americans have demonstrated their capacity to change institutions and values continuously and dramatically, when necessary. Countries around the globe have broadly accepted and imitated many American values and institutions.

NEW MODELS OF AMERICAN SOCIETY

The models that once worked, however, seem to have lost their power. The melting-pot, affirmative action, and industrial-era models—which guided American society's earlier social, philosophical, and organizational transformations—prove inappropriate to today's needs.

From Melting Pot to Salad Bowl

American culture has long espoused the melting-pot model of assimilation: Immigrants and minority populations blend into the general population and eventually become successful in the majority culture. But, for a variety of reasons, America's inner cities have lost much of their capacity to provide opportunities for upward mobility. Moreover, the schools and other institutions that once unified citizens around American values have experienced a diminished capacity to do so.

Instead of a melting pot, America has become a salad bowl. Different groups have chosen to retain their customs and identity and not become fully assimilated. Some groups, once assimilated, now seek separation. And the number of groups laying claim to consideration under the rubric of cultural diversity is growing.

The melting-pot model assumes that all Americans aspire to a common culture and values. True, new populations left their imprints by changing the culture over time. But the metaphor of a common culture endured, and most citizens understood the components of common bonds. Today, that understanding is fraying. Confronted with the salad bowl model, Americans must pay greater attention to articulating and understanding their fundamental, common values while at the same time encouraging pluralism. Without the unifying focus of shared ideas, the proponents of cultural diversity tend to strengthen their particular constituent communities at the expense of "the community of communities."

From Affirmative Action to Removing Barriers

The affirmative action (civil rights) model promotes the protection of group rights and the establishment of social programs. Affirmative action programs have helped increase the numbers of minorities and women employed in the professions, government, and industry. Although affirmative action has substantially stimulated the growth of the minority middle class, it's proven less effective in supporting long-term economic gains for members of the minority underclass.

The model has shown its limitations in other ways as well. First, groups such as gays and lesbians, older workers, and those with physical challenges have tested the capacity of the affirmative action model to accord them protection and consideration.

Second, a backlash is brewing as opposition mounts against giving any special consideration based on group characteristics rather than on individual performance. Some of the backlash is ill-informed, mean-spirited, and even racist. Many people, however, oppose affirmative action on principle and point to examples of incompetent implementation.

Third, the growing heterogeneity of society makes group generalization difficult and even misleading. Simple categories don't adequately describe the racial and ethnic composition of the American population.

Moreover, no single position on any issue adequately represents the diversity of opinion among members of any racial, gender, or cultural group.

Noting these limitations, a number of organizations have moved beyond the affirmative action model. Their leaders employ one, some, or all of the following strategies:

- Engage in an unrelenting and continuing discussion of the shared values, accepted behaviors, and performance expectations of employees.
- Set high performance expectations.
- Discuss and analyze the barriers to individual performance that the organization's culture has created, often unwittingly, as the workforce has become more diverse.
- Redefine diversity beyond traditional racial, ethnic, and gender groups to include whatever affinity groupings make sense to the employees.
- Change the organization's culture to eliminate unreasonable barriers to performance and success.
- Reward people who understand and address the needs of increasingly diverse customers, and reward the leaders who create the environment where this can happen.
- Actively and persistently seek skillful individuals, from highly diverse backgrounds, who demonstrate the capacity to understand and meet high performance standards.

From Industrial Era to Information Era

Industrial-era organizations established bureaucracies and hierarchies that relied on a monolithic organizational culture, rules, and control systems to achieve their aims. People at the top orchestrated fundamental change and expected employees to fit into a single, stable organizational culture. This model enabled American industry, education, and government to establish preeminence during the 20th century.

In the 21st century, however, information has replaced industry as the driving force. Despite what the calendar says, the 1990s are the first decade of the 21st century. Today's organizations require flatter, less hierarchical, networked organizations so information can flow freely. They must be flexible, responsive, and continuously adaptive. The information-era model pushes decision making down in the organization, as close to the customer as possible. Today, an organization's success depends on world-class performance by empowered, skillful, committed teams drawn from a diverse workforce.

The information-era model requires greater organizational tolerance for pluralism. The demands of the marketplace shape organizational culture, making it a continually evolving entity. Front-line employees, those in contact with the customers, interpret and respond to those demands. In this setting, employers that deliver honesty, opportunity, and satisfying work can expect a higher level of commitment from their workers and greatly enhanced productivity.

BREAKING THE SHACKLES OF OLD MODELS

Although the old models have lost some of their transformative power, American institutions seem unable or unwilling to abandon them. Most remain stuck in old patterns of behavior for dealing with race, ethnicity, and gender and have difficulty dealing with new facets of diversity. Too, many minority groups find it difficult to expand, reshape, or abandon the old models as long as they have "unfinished business." Yet most human resource managers and organizational leaders realize that they need to add a new ingredient to accelerate progress.

In our research for this book, we noticed an interesting phenomenon: Organizations that are dealing with complex, multicultural environments enjoy greater success in meeting the needs of customers of dazzling diversity. They're also able to openly confront diversity challenges internally. The pattern repeats again and again: in the management of hotel properties on the East and West Coasts; in the staging of effective international meetings held in Europe, Asia, South America, and the United States; in selling insurance in California to clients who speak dozens of languages; and in sales representations to immigrant populations and minority communities across the country. In each case, the insights gained from dealing with the multicultural experience have proven instrumental to the organization's overall success.

Using Multiculturalism as a Guide

The essence of effective multicultural interaction is portrayed in *Managing in a Pluralistic Society* (Hamzah-Sendut, Madsen, and Thong Tin Sin, 1989), which describes how business is transacted within Malaysia's highly diverse society. While it's possible in Malaysia to do business with your own ethnic community exclusively, genuine success requires reaching out to other communities as partners and customers. So Chinese, Malay, expatriate (European), Indian, and Arab businesspeople must understand and deal effectively with people from many diverse cultures.

Conducting business successfully in a multicultural setting such as Malaysia requires commitment and hard work. You must demonstrate commitment to certain shared values of civility and respect for property and to the distinctive cultural values of your associates. Understanding these cultural values and preferences requires a continual learning process—you must work diligently to know the needs of your associates. Continually learning and demonstrating care and respect are part of the *quid pro quo* of successful international interactions.

The principles for succeeding in multicultural settings apply in domestic settings as well. We found them at work in North American hotel properties and in businesses dealing with multicultural customers. The three principles are:

1. People from different cultures interact most effectively when all parties "have their antennae out"—when they demonstrate a concern for the cultural sensitivities and values of the other parties. Everyone must be in a learning mode.
2. Paying attention to someone's needs demonstrates respect, not just understanding. It reflects an appreciation of the power of that person as a customer or a partner. Respect conveyed leads to respect returned.
3. When bringing together people from different cultures, organizations are most effective when they create a new culture that's an amalgamation, rather than accept a predominant culture from one of the groups. People in the organization should "own" this amalgamated culture and continuously explore its shared values and expectations.

These principles illuminate the limitations of the earlier American models. Too often, managers operating on the old models ask for greater effort or understanding from some groups than others. This leads group members to feel, "I've always had to know about you; it's time you learned about *me*." Leaders of such organizations tend to treat people of difference as powerless clients rather than as customers or partners. Internally, these leaders usually require people of difference to fit into an existing predominant culture that fails to adapt. By taking this narrow approach, they avoid finding a basis for broader ownership.

Applying the lessons learned from the international, multicultural experience can certainly improve the way American businesses address diversity and interact with a diverse clientele. These skills are essential to success in the global workplace of the 21st century.

MAKING THE MARKETPLACE ARGUMENT

You've undoubtedly heard the two mainstream arguments for valuing diversity in the United States. The moral argument says, "It's the right thing to do," and the workforce argument says, "Get with the program. That's who your future workers will be."In the 21st century, American organizations will draw their employees from an increasing number of ethnic and racial minorities, women, people with disabilities, immigrants, single parents, and other people of difference. To attract the best employees, organizations must position themselves as good places to work.

But there's a more compelling argument for diversity and inclusiveness: success in the marketplace. The organizations that are winning with diversity have found that the marketplace argument is the most powerful instrument for continual, pervasive organizational change and adaptation. Being inclusive helps organizations to better understand and serve their customers. It also enables them to leverage differences and thus gain competitive advantage. The capacity to capitalize on changing demographic conditions in the marketplace becomes a fundamental core competency of the organization.

The marketplace argument for diversity plays out distinctively in different settings. For example:

- The **American Association of University Women** (AAUW) embraced diversity to redefine itself. It implemented a radical marketing plan that included targeting men and women of different racial, ethnic, economic, physical, and cultural backgrounds. AAUW's leaders crafted a multicultural environment to set an example for their constituents and to allow staff to thrive. Their success debunks the myth that addressing inclusiveness is for white men only.

- The **Westin Hotel in Seattle** attracts diverse clients because it provides service tailored to their needs. Employees are multicultural and are schooled in serving multicultural clients.

- **Ortho Biotech, Inc.**, a pharmaceutical subsidiary of Johnson & Johnson, operates in a fast-moving field. To remain competitive, Ortho Biotech needed to achieve a level of flexibility and productivity beyond the industry standard. To achieve employee commitment to this high level of performance, Ortho Biotech reshaped its corporate culture to value diversity, systematically eliminated barriers to performance, and created shared ownership of the corporate culture, values, and business goals.

- Members of the **Society for Human Resource Management** (SHRM)—human resource managers—are responsible for promulgating the concepts of diversity and inclusiveness in their employing organizations. To capitalize on the importance of these concepts, SHRM must take the lead in defining the field and understanding its distinctive application in the variety of settings represented by its members. Otherwise, competing providers may steal SHRM's thunder and preclude it from attaining a new stature for itself and its members.

- At the **Allstate Insurance Company**, corporate leaders understand that different cultures have dramatically different insurance requirements and expectations. To succeed in the marketplace, local offices must deal effectively and sensitively with different languages, cultures, and needs. Allstate leaders consciously manage diversity as a means of understanding and serving a dramatically changing customer base, capturing new markets, increasing customer satisfaction, and retaining customers.

- To be seen as successful, the **United Way of America** (UWA) must demonstrate its capacity to do good works for all segments of the community. To ensure the client populations of its member agencies received effective services, United Way began attracting more minorities and people of difference as board members and volunteers for local offices and member agencies. Furthermore, the system had to take note: Minorities and other people of difference provide money to the philanthropic organizations that are sensitive to their needs.

- **Girl Scouts of the U.S.A.** (GSUSA) faced diminishing membership and financial resources as the demography of America changed and it remained a white, middle-class organization. After years of extensively promoting diversity and reaching out to all communities, GSUSA has institutionalized pluralism. Its membership and staff reflect the diversity of America. GSUSA's key goal: Make everyone feel valued and recognize the benefits of inclusion.

(For more detailed explanations of these organizations' efforts, see Chapters 2 through 9.)

Typically, those responsible for introducing diversity programs into an organization must first convince executive leadership that diversity is worth the effort. If they can make compelling workforce and marketplace arguments for diversity, this difficulty disappears. Moreover, if the leaders understand that the ultimate result of managing diversity is establishing competitive advantage, they will ensure that all diversity initiatives are taken seriously.

THE STAGES OF DIVERSITY DEVELOPMENT

No two organizations approach diversity in the same manner. In most organizations, diversity programs have been the responsibility of human resource staff and have evolved from affirmative action programs. In some organizations, continuous quality improvement (CQI) programs and customer-service initiatives have also addressed the challenges presented by diverse workforces and customers. Often they have reached the same conclusions about cultural change and inclusiveness that resulted from the diversity-driven perspective. Ultimately, when these initiatives merge, diversity becomes a mainstream instrument of management.

In examining the organizations profiled in this handbook, we developed a framework to show how the components of diversity evolve. (Exhibit 3 outlines the stages of diversity development. Appendix A explains this framework in greater detail, describing how the strategy, tactics, and tools change at each stage.)

Stage I: Affirmative Action. At this stage, the diversity goal focuses on recruiting and supporting the advancement of targeted groups that are underrepresented in the marketplace. The primary tools of affirmative action are establishing hiring and retention goals, compliance reporting, recruiting, and consciousness raising. "Doing the right thing" and government mandates provide the rationale for affirmative action. Commitment can be superficial; opposition is often hidden or even subliminal. Affirmative action is usually seen as an initiative or program driven by the human resource staff.

EXHIBIT 3 - THE STAGES OF DIVERSITY DEVELOPMENT

Characteristic	Affirmative Action	Valuing Diversity	Managing Diversity	Building Inclusive, High-Performing Organizations
Diversity Goals	• Recruit from targeted, underrepresented groups in the workforce. • Support and maintain their advancement.	• Understand and value the contributions of people of difference.	• Develop an understanding of managing diversity to establish competitive advantage.	• Eliminate barriers to performance based on superficial differences. • Establish high standards. • Establish competitive advantage.
Leadership Commitment	• Commitment can be superficial. Hidden opposition based on personal values.	• Commitment is uneven, depending on the personal values of individuals.	• Commitment increases as the marketplace linkage becomes understood.	• Commitment is total and pervasive.
Status in the Organization	• Affirmative action (AA) is seen as a special initiative or program, driven by human resource management.	• Valuing diversity is an initiative or program with a human resource focus.	• Managing diversity is a new management perspective. Human resource management increasingly involves line management in developing the concept.	• Building inclusiveness is a fundamental value of the organization, not an initiative. • Central to organizational strategy.
Rationale	• Moral argument. • Government mandates.	• Moral argument. • Workforce argument for diversity.	• Workforce argument for diversity. • Understanding the marketplace argument for diversity.	• Marketplace and workforce arguments for diversity. • Use inclusiveness to establish competitive advantage.
Primary Tools	• Hiring goals and compliance reporting, recruiting. • Consciousness raising.	• Diversity training. • Communications, recognition days, and other celebrations of diversity.	• Diversity training integrated into everyone's professional development. • Assessing and changing the organizational culture to eliminate barriers.	• Continual cultural change. • Inclusiveness, team building, continuous quality improvement, and empowerment. • Measurement of success.

Stage II: Valuing Diversity. While continuing its affirmative action activities, the organization begins to focus on understanding and valuing the contributions of people of difference. The primary tools for this stage are diversity training and consciousness raising. Other tools include publications and meetings that convey the value of diversity, ethnic recognition days, and other celebrations of diversity.

The work starts with the leaders but ultimately includes much of the organization. Depending on their personal values, leaders may have an uneven commitment. The link between valuing diversity and success in the marketplace is weak, but understanding is building. Valuing diversity, which remains a human resource staff function, is still viewed as a special program or initiative.

Stage III: Managing Diversity. People in organizations at this stage begin to genuinely understand the power and potential of winning with diversity. The organization moves from merely valuing diversity to understanding how managing diversity can contribute to competitive advantage. The primary tools shift from diversity training to an assessment of organizational culture, followed by a progressive, systematic elimination of barriers to performance.

Although the workforce argument serves as the primary rationale for diversity, at this stage the leaders begin to see the link between diversity and success in the marketplace. The commitment grows as the link becomes clearer. As performance and behavioral expectations reflect this link, the commitment of rank-and-file employees also grows. While human resource staff still take the lead, line managers increasingly take ownership of the concept.

This is a transitional stage that can last for years; it takes time for staff to develop the skills needed to move to the next stage of development. But this is the point where organizations really begin to win with diversity.

Stage IV: Building an Inclusive, High-Performing Organization. The primary diversity goal at this stage is establishing an inclusive organization that has a genuine competitive advantage in the marketplace. The primary tools are continual cultural assessment and change, although the organization continues team building, empowerment, and continuous quality improvement activities. Everyone in the organization fully understands the marketplace and workforce arguments for diversity. Performance and behavioral measures for all employees reflect this understanding. Leadership commitment is total and pervasive: Building inclusiveness has become a fundamental value of the organization and a part of mainstream management.

The organizations studied for this handbook represent various levels of development. Most are either at the valuing diversity stage and transitioning to managing diversity, or they're at the managing diversity stage and transitioning to building an inclusive, high-performing organization. The most advanced organizations have begun to build the competencies and experience necessary to move into the final stage of development.

WINNING WITH DIVERSITY IN THE 21ST CENTURY

The United States—and the rest of the world—will continue to face the major challenge of diversity well into the 21st century. Around the globe, organizations that develop the capacity to understand and address the needs of diverse employees and customers will find themselves well-positioned to succeed.

Managing diversity will soon become fully integrated with other key concepts of 21st century management: team building, empowerment, and continuous quality improvement. Diversity will cease being a stand-alone program or initiative. But during the transition, it will be important for organizations to focus on understanding, valuing, and managing diversity and to introduce these concepts as core competencies.

MAKING MEETINGS USEFUL FOR EVERYONE

Meeting professionals—and the groups to which they belong— can make a dramatic difference in establishing an organization's reputation. Every event they stage tells the world how well a particular organization is faring in its efforts to embrace diversity.

It's hard work, meeting professionals will tell you, and you can't always get everything right. But staging an event that's both useful and inclusive can become the norm. What it takes is a committed staff that increases its awareness of diversity issues and obtains ongoing and proper training.

Although a number of global corporations and planning organizations do a superb job of recognizing multiculturalism abroad and embracing diversity domestically, we've developed a fictional company named Global Meetings, Inc. This composite profile provides a more complete example of how a meeting planning organization can lead the way to diversity and inclusiveness.

COMPOSITE STUDY

GLOBAL MEETINGS, INC. (GMI)
Showcasing Diversity at the Rendezvous

Last year alone, our composite company Global Meetings, Inc. (GMI) posted $8.5 million in earnings. Domestic (U.S.) endeavors with multicultural groups generated slightly more than half of the earnings, with the remainder coming from international projects conducted in the United States and abroad. The staff (15 full-time, six part-time, and four to eight consultants) have cultivated the company's worldwide reputation for excellence.

Like many of its counterparts in the United States, GMI's mission is to provide high-quality service that exceeds the client's expectations. Unlike most organizations, however, GMI invests significant resources in achieving competitive advantage by valuing diversity. But the leaders don't call these efforts "valuing diversity" or anything similar. The president says setting and meeting high standards for customer satisfaction, developing inclusive publications, maintaining a motivated and diverse staff, and helping other planning organizations improve is simply "the way we do business."

Setting the Scene for Satisfaction

GMI's staff always intertwines their efforts to make meetings useful and to make customers comfortable. GMI managers assign experienced meeting professionals to projects—people who won't make a major faux pas or cultural assumptions about the group being hosted. Staff always remain open to learning; they dig deep to determine exactly what each customer wants and needs to feel at home.

To keep track of client requests, GMI staff developed a checking system. A client checklist details the options available to the meeting sponsor, while an attendee checklist helps GMI develop an attendee profile. Other comprehensive checklists outline the features and options of the service providers, vendors, and facilities to be used for the client. GMI staff have discovered that the more information they elicit up front, the more quickly they can identify the most appropriate accommodations and support.

Once the client has completed its wish list (GMI's checklist), staff use other lists to complete the following:

- **Plan a program.** During this phase staff consider cultural and religious expectations, family involvement, amenities, and services. When hosting international meetings they factor in the effects of operating in a multiple-language environment. For example, they allot extra time for networking and breaks, set appropriate start and end times, and find ways to ease tension resulting from language barriers.

- **Visit and choose a site.** Staff determine how well the attendees will be accepted, site accessibility and reputation, and whether multilingual staff and interpreters are available (if necessary).

- **Promote the event.** For all meetings, domestic and international, GMI staff scrutinize publications and documents for clarity: The attendees should assume nothing. For meetings with international clients, GMI factors in additional lead time for translation of materials.

- **Select food and service.** The planners look carefully at the attendee profile before selecting menus, setting meal times, and determining whether and when to provide alcoholic beverages.

To help with the planning, GMI even has a protocol for tracking down local contacts with knowledge of sites, resources, and vendors. When necessary, GMI staff also double check logistics with their counterparts at home and abroad. When in doubt, planners rely on other resources. In fact, on every planner's desk you'll find two texts: *Managing Diversity: A Complete Desk Reference and Planning Guide* (Gardenswartz and Rowe, 1993) and *Conducting International Meetings* (The GWSAE Foundation, 1993).

Beyond merely meeting clients' articulated needs GMI staff draw on the experience they've gained in a wide variety of multicultural settings. As a result, staff pride themselves on raising clients' consciousness of diversity and inclusiveness issues that may have been overlooked in the past. GMI markets this value-added concept as one of its core competencies.

Speaking the Language of Diversity or Talking the Talk

Because the company stages events in major cities worldwide, it has complex communications systems. The publications and communications staff must not only be sensitive to difference but also adhere to an editorial policy that emphasizes accuracy and cultural appropriateness. The policy applies to all materials, from memos and brochures to promotional items and transcripts. Additionally, for international events, a language expert and a practitioner of the trade or profession review the materials.

GMI's electronic capabilities include electronic mail, teleconferencing, videoconferencing, simultaneous translation, audio and video services, and more should the client request it. Staff ensure that GMI's headquarters as well as any meeting site can handle multiple methods of language translation and interpretation. All locations can handle incoming and outgoing fax transmissions, phone calls, and other communications from remote locations.

GMI is most proud of the many languages spoken by its staff. This has proved the company's ace in the hole, ensuring its ease in dealing with diversity and multiculturalism. Again and again, staff claim they feel at home at any site—and they know how to make customers feel at home, too.

The communications director plans to expand the staff's diversity library with a book tentatively titled *Multiculturalism and the Meeting Professional*. GMI employees will coauthor the book, which will detail GMI's best practices for making meetings useful and comfortable for everyone.

Getting Staff Commitment

The staff's diversity at GMI's headquarters and at meeting sites always impresses visitors. Differences are evident at all levels, from support staff to management, sending a subtle message to all would-be applicants: If you want to work only with people who look, speak, and act like you, apply elsewhere. Conversely, the people who work at GMI want an environment that "feels like it promotes independent thinking, individuality, and creativity," says the receptionist.

Still, you'd find some thorns among the roses. The receptionist says that most of the staff think it's great to have people who are different working together. Whenever opinions and styles of communicating differ, however, tension builds. A year ago, GMI's leaders hired a consultant to devise conflict-resolution programs; the number of disagreements has decreased. Also, all GMI employees participate in ongoing diversity training sessions. The managers receive additional training in forming diverse work teams, encouraging an inclusive culture, and hiring and promoting people based on their ability to be inclusive.

"GMI doesn't just hire highly credentialed, bilingual people to make the corporate capability statement look good," says one manager. Another adds, "We look for people who want to work in a multicultural environment. In an interview, we pay attention to how they describe people, if they make derogatory remarks about others, and if they tend to stereotype people." If the qualifications for working at GMI seem rigorous, management quickly points out that the company also offers an excellent benefits package. Recently, for example, GMI authorized several job-sharing arrangements for new parents on staff.

Raising Others' Consciousness

For several years, GMI has conducted consciousness-raising seminars at the annual conference of Meeting Professionals International (MPI). When asked if GMI's goal to spur other association members to action would eventually hurt GMI by creating stiff competition, the vice president of operations emphatically answered "NO!" Besides, she added, "while they're getting good, we'll be getting better." She also believes untold opportunities await meeting professionals who respect difference and provide world-class service. "In our line of work," she says, "we can explore new frontiers in terms of going where we've never gone before and doing what we've never done."

For MPI's 1994 annual conference banquet, four GMI staff members took on new roles. One posed as a male from Cameroon; he wore native attire and spoke limited English. Another was a visually impaired British female dressed in a formal evening gown. Two other employees, white American males wearing tuxedos, served as the control group. During the awards ceremony—without mentioning any names—GMI described how the meeting professionals attending the conference had fared on basic tests of kindness, consideration, and helpfulness.

The results? Not surprisingly, the American males had a grand time throughout the conference. Other attendees inundated them with business cards, proposals, and requests for information. Both the woman and the other man were ignored from day one. Her requests for assistance were met with impatience and occasionally discourteous behavior—even from hotel staff. MPI as an organization received low marks for not having a committee to greet and welcome newcomers and for choosing a site where the seminar rooms had poor lighting and acoustics. The conference presenters included 10 white males and two females—the latter leading sessions on "Dressing for Success" and "Pack It Quickly, Pack It Lightly."

In addition to announcing the disappointing results of their role play, GMI staff reminded attendees what makes for a stellar meeting: the care and attention to detail that meeting professionals provide. Qualified employees who receive ongoing training in an environment that supports diversity can make sure meetings are useful and comfortable for everyone. Key strategies include creating a detailed attendee profile and selecting a good site staffed with good people.

PRACTICAL APPLICATIONS

Meeting professionals working for international firms and domestic associations know that a useful meeting is a carefully planned meeting. It's key to have a sensitive staff capable of handling multiple duties and eliciting the right information at the right time. They also need to know the profile and preferences of potential attendees, how best to meet attendees' needs, and the ins and outs of potential sites and surrounding areas.

Both in the United States and abroad, people demand the most for their dollar (or austral or pound or markka). The following tips, distilled from the composite study and vignettes in Chapters 2 through 9, can help you meet that demand.

LESSONS LEARNED

- Hosting an inclusive meeting means paying attention to details throughout the planning phase; working with knowledgeable sources to avoid offending anyone; and using service providers, vendors, and facilities that reflect diversity. Your service partners must share your commitment to and skills in dealing with diversity.
- Whenever possible, expand the number of options available to attendees regarding style of dress, menu selections, and entertainment. Checklists that itemize options and preferences for the client and attendee also help simplify the planner's job and ensure a good outcome.
- The inclusiveness-oriented meeting professional does more than just respond to a client's needs; he or she helps the client understand emerging diversity-driven needs that haven't yet been articulated. Planning personnel should be flexible, willing to deal with diverse people, and able to juggle multiple tasks and match a multitude of preferences.
- Electronic mail (E-mail) simplifies communication. Whenever possible, companies should be linked electronically. The advantages include simplifying work with multiple cultures and time zones and communicating with people who have hearing impairments.

HELPFUL HINTS

Getting Started

- **Make understanding diversity and inclusiveness a priority.** Win your CEO's commitment to these issues and their importance to your success in the marketplace. Make certain your organization regularly and effectively communicates that commitment.
- **Join networks of meeting professionals.** Become connected so you can stay on top of changes and activities in your industry. Include diverse associations or groups of meeting professionals in your network.

- **Ask the right questions of meeting attendees and employees.** For example: "How can we make our meetings more inclusive, comfortable, and useful?" Make this a standard question on your meeting evaluation form and a regular topic of discussion in staff meetings.
- **Be sensitive to differences at all times.** Make sure the plans for the program and the presenters reflect the differences among the organization, staff, members, and attendees.
- **Include diversity training as part of staff development and training.** Require all staff to participate, but don't treat the training as a special initiative.
- **Pay attention to site selection, set design, and time.** Choose sites in areas that can accommodate attendees' preferences, tastes, and needs. Make sure the site can design settings that promote inclusion, such as using comfortable seats and seating arrangements and appropriate equipment (large screens, for example). Time meetings, seminars, workshops, and breaks to start and end for the convenience of attendees.
- **Be sensitive to food and beverage choices.** Make sure your sites can accommodate special diets. Limit alcohol consumption and carefully select the type of snacks and beverages and the times they're offered.
- **Make all guests feel welcome.** Pay special attention to newcomers. People with special needs shouldn't feel singled out.
- **Develop and distribute preregistration/preconference information.** In the materials give detailed instructions and descriptions of the local culture. Tell attendees what they need to know to be comfortable.
- **During the meeting, schedule at least one session that deals with diversity in a practical setting.** Use this opportunity to educate attendees about how issues of diversity and inclusion affect different parts of your industry or profession.
- **Consider attendee preferences.** Adjust services and actions according to the type of conference, type of participants, age groups, nationality, and cultural background. For example, take vacation times, standard office hours, and dates into consideration when planning the meeting. For specific events, think about the attendees' comfort—their need for breaks, refreshments, and lively sessions.
- **Take advantage of technological advances.** Use closed-caption projections, good sound systems, and big screens to ensure the satisfaction and comfort of customers and guests.
- **Devise a checklist for evaluating sites.** Ask people with physical disabilities to help you determine if a site is truly friendly to those who use wheelchairs, have seeing-eye dogs, or have difficulty communicating.
- **Devise a checklist guests and customers can use to indicate special needs and preferences.** Specify accommodations and special technolo-

gies, such as closed-captioned projections, for those who are physically challenged. Also include dietary restrictions, communication needs (interpretation, translation, teleconferencing, or computer services), and financial concerns (banking and exchange procedures).

- **Sponsor or develop programs for subgroups of attendees.** Organizations profiled in this handbook not only develop programs for spouses and children but also offer vegetarian, Kosher, and international menus. Some even develop directories of local hot spots, ethnic events and exhibits, and so forth.

- **Develop satisfaction surveys to elicit comments from attendees.** Document your efforts so you can track what you've tried, what works, and what doesn't.

- **Start a diversity library and clip file.** Ask your staff to remain on the look-out for books and articles on diversity and meeting planning. For additional recommendations, see Appendix B.

Maintaining the Effort

- **Take advantage of E-mail.** Become connected with other meeting professionals and organizations and use this medium for scheduling, planning, and keeping abreast of changes. Use E-mail as a means of delivering messages at meetings and events.

- **Stay connected with other groups and associations.** Use your contacts with diverse associations and meeting professionals to develop a resource library and talent roster.

- **Form a "do it right" committee.** The committee, composed of diverse employees, should investigate potential meeting sites and evaluate issues or concerns raised by staff and attendees.

- **Develop a detailed checklist for evaluating sites.** Determine the characteristics of a site that promotes inclusion and therefore deserves your business. Circulate this information within your organization and to diverse meeting professionals. This will simplify the process of determining the suitability of locations.

- **Build a reputation for being inclusive.** Share your success stories in internal and industry-wide newsletters, magazines, and other media.

- **Develop your pool of resources.** Identify consultants who can help you tailor programs to solve the problems in your environment. Also identify several speakers to use as presenters at meetings or in house to keep staff up-to-date on diversity issues.

- **Make diversity training part of the regular training for meeting planning.** Staff shouldn't consider diversity training a separate initiative—it's part of preparing for business.

- **Continually scan the environment for information on issues affecting meeting planning.** Think ahead. Become a substantial resource for your members or clients on diversity and lifestyle issues that affect meetings. Challenge them to expand their horizons to establish a marketplace advantage.

- **Make each meeting a learning opportunity for all attendees.** Determine what concepts regarding multiculturalism and inclusiveness you will feature. After each meeting, calculate what percentage of attendees got the message; commit to increasing that percentage at future meetings.
- **Assess your decision-making processes.** Which teams make critical decisions about particular meetings and about organizational strategy? Are they diverse? Can you trace any bad decisions back to monocultural decision makers?

VIGNETTES

The experiences of these three corporations illustrate the many ways that meeting professionals are recognizing multiculturalism in international meetings. They also underscore the role staff play in making meetings useful for everyone.

Hosting Corporate Meetings for an International Workforce

ZENECA PHARMACEUTICALS

ZENECA Pharmaceuticals is part of ZENECA Group Plc, which researches, manufactures, and markets ethical pharmaceutical products. Headquartered in Cheshire, England, with research laboratories in the United States and France, ZENECA Pharmaceuticals has more than 12,000 employees worldwide and a customer base of medical specialists and healthcare providers in every country in the world. In 1993, ZENECA Group Plc reported sales of $6.57 billion (U.S.).

The majority of ZENECA meetings involve staff members or physicians from several countries. Although most come from western countries (England, France, United States, and Canada), a few are from further afield (Asia and South America). The need to accommodate cross-cultural diversity in meetings is a natural requirement for any international organization and has been common practice at ZENECA over the last decade. Often, it's a matter of common sense.

ZENECA places a high importance on staff attitude, flexibility, and willingness to deal sympathetically with other nationalities. In many cases, conference staff have traveled widely and know delegates and staff from other countries in social settings. The company provides language-training courses and cultural-awareness programs. E-mail makes for easy communication among ZENECA companies and helps break down barriers.

ZENECA's organizers recognize multiculturalism by paying close attention to site selection and time issues. For instance, the meeting site should have easy access from an international airport. Agencies or destination management companies accustomed to dealing with mixed groups should be available. As for hotels, they must be accustomed to international travelers and have facilities for the disabled, a multilingual staff, leisure facilities, good meeting rooms, imaginative banquet proposals, and the ability to produce different styles of food. Food and beverage service, if handled incorrectly, probably offers the most potential for offending people. Therefore, staff always bear in mind the particular preferences of different nationalities and religions.

ZENECA organizers usually use the 24-hour clock to schedule events, unless the group is exclusively American or Canadian. Timing can be a big problem with a group consisting of different nationalities. For example, the Americans may want the health club opened at 6 a.m. and be quite happy to start the meeting at 8 a.m. They also would prefer to be served dinner at 6:30 p.m. Spaniards, however, would prefer lunch at 14.00 and dinner at 21.00. ZENECA organizers compromise on a middle road and start dinner between 19.30 and 20.00.

Organizers have learned to consider other attendee preferences. In many countries, people take one month's vacation during the summer and offices close for the entire month of August. Therefore, ZENECA mails materials by mid-July and doesn't expect responses until mid-September. They also consider that standard office hours can vary and always double check dates. (Europeans write dates in order of day/month/year; Americans write month/day/year).

While acknowledging that no issue is too trivial, ZENECA staff refrain from overemphasizing issues. For example, they've found that emphasizing gender differences can cause resentment in a professional business setting. As a result, they balance their meetings to suit both sexes. Because 90 percent of ZENECA's meeting participants are between the ages of 30 and 50, the organizers have found no need for special physical activity arrangements, provided the meeting facility has adequate exercise facilities.

In addition, they make sure that all written documents are clear and unambiguous. That means avoiding the use of colloquialisms and using a layout that helps rather than hinders delivery of the message. This attention to detail and awareness of inclusiveness issues have earned ZENECA planners high marks from conference participants.

Staging Exhibitions and Conferences in a Multicultural Setting
Singapore Exhibition Services Pte Ltd (SES)

Singapore Exhibition Services (SES) is part of The Montgomery Network of international exhibition organizers, managers, and consultants. Its 42 employees specialize in organizing trade and business exhibitions and conferences. Staff take pride in creating effective platforms for buyers and sellers to meet and generate business. Their worldwide customer base includes such industries as oil, gas, petrochemicals, instrumentation and controls, environmental management, manufacturing, telecommunications, broadcasting, woodworking, food processing, and consumer goods.

In terms of comfort and facilities, SES has found most facilities in Singapore and Asia adequately equipped because of the multiracial population. The diverse, international character of the delegates attending SES conferences often creates the need for simultaneous interpretation and ethnic food service. SES often bases its selection of a venue or hotel on "basic comforts"—air conditioning, space and ambience, food-and-beverage service, and budget.

All SES meetings are in the English language. Because the multiracial population largely uses English as the language of business, communication doesn't present a serious problem for domestic conferences and meetings.

When scheduling exhibitions and conferences, organizers must account for the behavioral patterns of the country and industries. This includes choosing the proper day, date, or time, one that doesn't conflict with the many ethnic or religious holidays prevalent in Singapore and Asia. For example, in predominantly Muslim countries, SES avoids 11.00 to 14.00 on Fridays. In heavily Chinese communities, SES doesn't schedule meetings for the two weeks before and after Chinese New Year.

SES staff have found timing to be a critical issue. For example, a production machinery exhibition will do well straddling a weekend if it's held in Kuala Lumpur, Malaysia. The weekend timing allows rural participants to make the trip to Kuala Lumpur. The same timing, however, doesn't do well in Singapore, where the five-day work week is more deeply ingrained than in Malaysia.

Consider the following actions when planning your next event. They have helped SES increase attendance at conferences and exhibitions:

- Make provisions for a preregistration facility to avoid an opening-day queue. This also enables SES to give attendees advance information and advice, including the dress code and directions to facilities.
- Use a registration system that accepts both cash and credit payments.
- Set up a messaging system that includes notice boards as a central message point and uses electronic, computerized mail boxes.
- Intersperse hands-on workshop sessions throughout the conference.
- Schedule postconference tours and activities, when feasible.
- Develop interesting programs for people accompanying participants.
- Ask participants to evaluate speakers on charisma, subject matter, and so forth.

Planning Inclusive Meetings

CONGRESS INTERNACIONALES, S.A.

Congress Internacionales is a professional congress organizer and independent meeting planning company in Buenos Aires, Argentina. Associations, corporations, and other private businesses represent its main clientele. The seven full-time and five part-time employees organize an average of 15 meetings per year, of which 60 percent are international, 20 percent are national, and 20 percent are corporate. Conferences range from 100 to 3,000 participants and last from three to four days. The company operates on an annual budget of $3 million to $5 million, with net revenues between $250,000 and $500,000.

Inclusiveness is a priority for Congress Internacionales, which tries to deliver universal messages without disrespecting social, racial, or religious differences. Because the staff have roots in many different races and cultures, they haven't received any special training. The company belongs to the Organization of International Conferences, which requires its members to ensure no discrimination occurs.

Congress Internacionales takes several measures to overcome language barriers. It provides simultaneous translation, signposting in other languages, bilingual or trilingual staff, and international catering services when organizing a social event. Inclusiveness issues drive the selection of meeting sites, which must be equipped for the disabled and provide non-smoking accommodations.

CHAPTER 3

MAKING CUSTOMERS COMFORTABLE AND SATISFIED

A link between succeeding in the marketplace and providing customers with comfort and satisfaction clearly exists. Hospitality and meetings-related organizations, as well as highly customer-sensitive corporations, have taken the lead in showing that managing diversity is essential to pleasing customers. They have linked formal diversity programs with aggressive, customer-driven initiatives.

The two case studies that follow illustrate these principles in action. The first discusses how Westin Hotels and Resorts has stimulated diversity programs in its hotel properties across the country. The second case study describes the Allstate Insurance Company's efforts to develop corporate diversity initiatives linked to marketplace forces. Local sales offices have played a critical role in demonstrating how to win with diversity.

CASE STUDY

WESTIN HOTELS AND RESORTS

Prodding All Properties to Win with Diversity

Despite myriad differences, the 35 properties that make up Westin Hotels and Resorts share one item—a how-to manual on managing diversity. Developed at corporate headquarters, the comprehensive 48-page *Diversity Planning Guide* helps managers set and reach the following goals:

1. Ensure that business is conducted in a way that reflects the diversity of employees and customers.
2. Enable people to maximize their talents and provide superior service.
3. Create an atmosphere boasting unsurpassed appreciation for the diversity of race, heritage, religion, age, and other characteristics of employees, guests, and business associates.

Developing a culture that values diversity, corporate leaders believe, takes strong leadership, a formal structure, and resources. Among the most important activities of leaders are reaching consensus on how to implement a diversity plan, determining appropriate behaviors needed to model leadership, and understanding the relationship of leadership and other management responsibilities to winning with diversity.

At a minimum, each property needs a diversity planning committee, a diversity administrator, and a strategic plan to organize and orchestrate its diversity effort. Such a structure sets the parameters for implementation roles and responsibilities. Additionally, it's key for each property to determine the availability of people committed to the diversity effort and identify the money, time, and information needed to sustain the effort.

Although different properties may address different concerns, Westin's corporate leaders believe all properties should deal with diversity issues involving communication, training, rewards, and measurements. These include, for example, developing effective communication strategies that ensure everyone understands the need for the diversity initiative, knows his or her role during implementation, and understands Westin's commitment to and policies supporting diversity.

Furthermore, training is equally important for all employees. The corporation's leaders believe initial training should create awareness of the diversity that exists on the particular property. Later trainings should challenge employees to value diversity and then to better manage diversity. Rewards and recognition reinforce each property's achievements. Westin's leaders also believe predetermined measurements enable managers to monitor progress in meeting diversity goals. As a result, each hotel's human resource director—or the diversity administrator—is evaluated on the basis of his or her ability to manage and understand diversity. Each property manager has the responsibility for developing a plan tailored to the property. Westin encourages managers to share information regularly; think proactively; and continuously improve their ability to serve Westin's guests, employees, and business associates.

Here's how the process has played out at two properties.

The Westin Hotel in Seattle (WHS): So far, three out of four staff members have received diversity training. The new employee orientation program deals with diversity issues, and diversity statements appear in advertisements and the employee handbook.

The human resource staff places the property in the valuing diversity stage of development. Its customer-service orientation has driven WHS far along the diversity continuum. Seattle is a genuinely cosmopolitan city; the Westin's staff is not only multicultural but also schooled in serving a multicultural clientele. For example, the front desk always has a Japanese-speaking person. The sales manager also speaks Japanese.

WHS recently hosted the Asian Pacific Economic Conference (APEC), whose attendees included government leaders from 15 countries. Before selecting the Westin, APEC checked on whether the property could prepare diverse menus and assist people who spoke many languages. WHS rose to the challenge, giving all housekeepers tags coded with the primary language they spoke (the hotel's staff cover 20 different languages). APEC also used AT&T's interpretation services, providing access to 125 languages via conference call.

The hotel's managers characterize their diversity effort as "doing what it takes to celebrate difference and giving people the opportunities to learn how to relate." The property sponsors a variety of programs and activities for staff, clients, and the community. For example, WHS pays for English classes for employees and created a housekeeping quality improvement team to foster teamwork and a better working relationship between shifts. Another team, consisting of continuous improvement coordinators, deals with internal communication between managers and associates and enables staff to evaluate managers.

For the community, WHS sponsors a Job Shadow Days program: Students at risk of dropping out of school spend the day learning about a hotel employee's job. WHS also participates in a Junior Achievement program.

WHS is poised to integrate its formal diversity program with its fundamental orientation to customer service, multicultural sensitivity, and continuous quality improvement initiatives.

The Westin Crown Center (WCC): This property has incorporated a diversity policy into its business plan. Managers and staff implemented the diversity effort, along with a Total Quality Management (TQM) initiative, over three years. The result? Numerous activities, services, and marketing strategies that invite an increasingly diverse clientele.

For example, WCC can meet guests' requests for custom menus (including Kosher and vegetarian) and translation services. The hotel publishes a foreign language directory and a list of staff members who speak other languages. In 1993 the hotel sponsored a "Day in the Life of . . ." lesson, which enabled hotel executives to experience firsthand the hotel's treatment of physically challenged guests.

WCC staff make no secret of placing diverse staff in key positions and programs at the hotel. Meeting planners can review documents that indicate employment trends and demonstrate the absence of discriminatory practices on site. As James Seay, director of human resources, says, "If you can't show representation, it will affect the meeting planner's decision."

WCC engenders the staff's commitment to diversity through teamwork, training, and feedback, all done with the goal of maximizing each person's full potential. All employees participate in quality improvement teams, where they develop ideas for customer service, cost savings, and safety. They also make a commitment to the hotel's service guarantee—to serve the customer and offer personalized service. These elements, which are part of WCC's mission statement, empower employees to do whatever they believe it takes to please guests.

Staff receive feedback through guest satisfaction surveys that rate items such as staff friendliness, quality of service, and overall value. At the managerial level, diversity training focuses on understanding differences and the cultures represented on the staff.

Case Study

Leveraging Differences in the Workplace and Marketplace

Since forming the Chairman's Diversity Management Committee in 1990, Allstate Insurance Company has developed ways to better respond to the needs of its 20 million customers and 14,500 employees throughout the United States and Canada. In 1993 the company appointed a Diversity Change Team and charged it with developing a strategy for managing diversity.

"Managing diversity is a business strategy for leveraging differences in the workplace to gain competitive advantage in the marketplace," say team members in their September 1994 update. They also define managing diversity according to the location and results achieved. In the workplace, managing diversity means creating a supportive environment that enables all employees to contribute their full potential. In the marketplace, it means creating growth and outperforming the competition by capitalizing on demographic changes.

The Diversity Change Team began by conducting a cultural audit and benchmarking survey, analyzing statistics related to Allstate's workforce and customer base, and examining human resource processes and demographic trends. These activities gave the team baseline measurements for tracking and comparison purposes. More important, the results helped the team devise this six-point plan:

1. Require members of the Senior Management Team to participate in education sessions and speak with employees on diversity issues.
2. Redesign employee selection and development practices.
3. Have leaders and employees learn managing diversity concepts, as well as how to manage and leverage differences, leverage commonalities, manage conflict, influence others, and assume responsibility.
4. Incorporate diversity concepts with customer interactions, such as advertising, point-of-sale materials, and marketplace activities.
5. Develop a variety of communication vehicles so leaders and employees can easily discuss workplace and marketplace topics. (For example, Allstate plans to introduce an 800-number that employees can use to talk about diversity-related subjects and to provide feedback to company leaders.)
6. In addition to the tracking of internal measurements of affirmative action results, survey results, and turnover rates, develop other diversity indicators. Compare these indicators with business results.

The Diversity Change Team sees managing diversity as a means of strengthening interactions with its employees and customers. Concurrent with the team's planning efforts, Allstate has initiated changes that involve employees, customers, communications, and communities.

Focusing on Employees

Allstate initially targeted leaders and managers as the audience for diversity workshops on communication and publications. But executives found that the program had to be for everyone, so diversity training has become part of the development process for all employees.

Allstate has focused on eliminating barriers to successful performance and advancement for all employees as well. Moreover, the company has developed measures of behavior that evaluate a person's ability to eliminate barriers and to support the success of diverse employees. Specifically, the company has invested considerable energy in articulating its organizational values—integrity, caring, initiative, and innovation. Associated with these values are a series of specific behaviors, such as "Eliminates behaviors based on personal prejudices," "Uses language and humor that don't demean others," and "Creates freedom and space for differences." Allstate operates on the premise that all successful employees need to embrace inclusiveness.

The human resource staff doesn't have the sole responsibility for addressing issues of diversity and inclusiveness. By linking workplace diversity to business objectives, Allstate has made diversity a major factor in its corporate strategy. Its approach is to foster a diverse environment that increases productivity, commitment, and innovation. Allstate also aims to understand and serve a changing customer base, capture new markets, increase customer satisfaction, and retain customers in the marketplace. These elements are the essence of competitive advantage.

Meeting the Needs of Customers

By the early 1990s, Allstate's leaders saw that demographics were changing marketplace opportunities and how the company needed to do business. Expanding the corporate diversity initiative—and linking it to the marketplace—corresponded to this awareness.

Change was especially evident in locations such as California and the Washington, D.C., metropolitan area, where handling claims and sales increasingly required cultural awareness and foreign language skills. Staff in the Washington area developed a directory listing nearly 50 languages and the employees who could speak and write in those languages. All sales locations in the region received a copy.

From Allstate's perspective, all employees must build relationships across differences of ethnicity, background, gender, age, and religious affiliations. As a result, it has never adopted a strategy of matching customers and salespeople—such as hiring Asians to penetrate the Asian market. Instead, Allstate hires employees who are courteous and knowledgeable, return phone calls, and show respect to all customers. At the same time, Allstate managers learned that employees don't want to be pigeonholed into a race, gender, or other classification category. They simply want to be valued and respected as productive employees.

Using Communications to Portray Diversity

Pictures of Allstate's workforce and leadership convey an image of diversity—because they are diverse. Local offices typically tailor their communications and sales materials to the needs and preferences of the local communities.

For its corporate publications, Allstate selects topics and themes that tie into its marketplace. For example, a piece entitled "Commitment to Urban America" portrays the company's commitment to improving urban neighborhoods and communities and describes strategic partnerships and investments in these areas.

Building the Community

Allstate's vision statement contains a commitment to society and the community. Any company wishing to build credibility as an inclusive organization must demonstrate this commitment.

Allstate does so in a variety of ways. It formed the Allstate Foundation to support community programs dealing with automobile and highway safety, homes and housing, and health and wellness. Allstate also has a Minority and Female Vendor Opportunity Program, which includes more than 1,500 suppliers in the United States, and supports an array of community partnerships and community service programs involving Allstate employees.

Looking Toward Tomorrow

Members of the Diversity Change Team believe successfully managing a diverse workforce and customer base are key to Allstate's long-term success. "Diversity has everything to do with our business," say team members, adding that Allstate must continue to address the changing needs of employees and customers to remain successful. Allstate has closely tied its initiative to manage diversity to its business goals of improving customer satisfaction, exceeding growth goals, and enhancing shareholder value.

PRACTICAL APPLICATIONS

Associations and hospitality enterprises have two sets of customers—employees and clients/internal and external—and have found they must satisfy the needs of both groups. Staff and managers of customer-oriented enterprises have learned a key point. Although people want their differences respected, they are most interested in being treated with respect.

LESSONS LEARNED

- There's no "cookie cutter" approach to implementing diversity initiatives and relating them to customer satisfaction. Each organization must determine the needs of its customers and fulfill their expectations. This requires constant surveillance and measurement.

- Good communication—which is a two-way process—is critical to customer comfort. Meeting professionals should see themselves as detectives: The more information they collect from their customers, the easier their job becomes and the more accurate their choices.
- Training staff to be sensitive to the needs of people of different backgrounds should be part of regular staff development exercises. Quite simply, that's the way to conduct business today.
- When meeting attendees see themselves represented in various roles throughout an event, their comfort level rises.

HELPFUL HINTS

Getting Started

- **Hire and promote staff based on customer-service potential and performance.** Beginning with the initial interview, emphasize the importance of understanding and serving customer needs. Include this expectation and inclusiveness-affirming behavior in performance reviews.
- **Train personnel to treat each customer respectfully and to determine the customer's needs and wants.** Diversity and inclusiveness should be a fundamental part of satisfying customer needs—not a special initiative.
- **Consider customer and attendee preferences.** Adjust services and actions according to the type of conference, type of participants, age groups, nationality, and cultural background. Consider vacations, standard office hours, and dates when planning the meeting. Also consider attendees' comfort—their need for breaks, refreshments, and short sessions.
- **Develop a protocol for making newcomers and customers feel welcome.** Have it in place at every gathering and every customer service setting.
- **Include detailed instructions and descriptions of local culture in all materials.** Omit any potentially offensive messages.
- **Select facilities, vendors, and service providers that comply with federal and state laws.** Be prepared to prove your own organization is in compliance with these laws as well as with any corporate ordinances. For example, maintain documents showing compliance with the Americans With Disabilities Act, a sexual harassment policy, and affirmative action guidelines. Update the policies that reflect your organization's commitment to diversity, and make them available for client review.
- **Begin creating a multicultural resource base.** Start with the names of diverse presenters and consultants, then use contacts with diverse meeting professionals to expand your list. Next, start a diversity library (See Appendix B for recommendations).

Maintaining the Effort

- **Continue to train staff and help them develop sensitivity to differences.** Provide cultural awareness training—in meeting hosting and customer service skills—to all levels of employees. Training shouldn't be viewed as a special initiative.
- **Scrutinize the composition of your staff.** Pay particular attention to those in front-line customer service and those who work at events. Make sure the diversity of the staff is equally represented in all levels of your organization and in different roles at events.
- **Assess how you make decisions regarding customer service.** Do you involve front-line customer service workers in those decisions? Do you use diverse teams? At all levels?
- **Regularly measure customer satisfaction.** Segment those measurements to determine if you're failing to satisfy particular portions of your customer base.
- **Tie customer satisfaction to employee performance.** Make customer evaluations part of performance reviews and compensation decisions. Reward individuals and teams for providing excellent customer service.
- **Have a protocol in place for identifying newcomers.** This goes beyond extending a welcome—it means substantially involving them in the proceedings and connecting them with key attendees.
- **Train staff members to demonstrate positive energy and think of possibilities.** Employees should be able to troubleshoot and solve problems, doing whatever it takes to respond to customers' requests and complaints.
- **Keep communication lines open.** Staff should know immediately where to go and who to talk to.
- **Continue expanding the resource pool.** Encourage staff to contribute ideas, clippings, and materials to build your library.
- **Stage practical learning opportunities.** Whenever possible, underscore your message—successfully operating in a multicultural environment is standard operating procedure—by exposing staff to hypothetical and real examples. Use a wide range of diversity characteristics and develop convincing examples of inclusiveness-affirming behavior.

Here are examples of how some organizations make their customers feel comfortable and satisfied.

Believing Every Customer Is Special

CONGRESS MANAGEMENT SYSTEMS

Congress Management Systems (CMS), a full-service professional congress organizer located in Helsinki, Finland, serves international association members and has an annual budget of $4 million. Two philosophies guide its seven-member staff: "Our customer is our king" and "Every customer is important and deserves to feel he or she is special."

To make meetings comfortable for everyone, CMS adjusts its services and actions according to the type of conference, type of participants, age groups, nationalities, and cultural backgrounds. Staff also read trade magazines and refer to the *Foreign Ministry Protocol Manual*. In difficult cases they consult the government's protocol department or specific associations.

Domestic and international meeting planning differ greatly, according to CMS staff. Issues and requirements that vary include the need for language interpretation; type of marketing and staff; selection of tours and social events, destinations, and venues; and special accommodations. The key for CMS is to provide detailed instructions and descriptions of local culture in all written materials. Some locations also require an awareness of government regulations, visa requirements, and entry blocks for certain nationalities. The staff's efforts to plan inclusive meetings have resulted in greater satisfaction among exhibitors and vendors, plus increased flexibility in their work.

Using Meetings to Demonstrate Commitment

NATIONAL ASSOCIATION OF SOCIAL WORKERS

The National Association of Social Workers (NASW), a professional society headquartered in Washington, D.C., initially addressed meetings and organizational culture with its diversity program. Leaders used local, regional, and national conferences to ensure their commitment to diversity was visible and taken seriously. Today all conferences include educational sessions on delivering social services to minorities.

The people who plan the agendas make sure each conference has a good representation of minority speakers, says Luisa Lopez, special assistant for affirmative action and affirmative action officer. Conferences always include networking time and space for the Latino, Asian-American, African-American, and other caucuses. These groups also place announcements in the conference brochure and are encouraged to identify issues and discuss goals for the whole association.

For minority social worker students, NASW provides opportunities for networking with practicing minority professionals. NASW also asks conference registrants to state any special needs and pays attention to the need for signers and wheelchairs.

Selecting Acceptable Meeting Sites

NATIONAL EDUCATION ASSOCIATION

The National Education Association (NEA), an advocacy and service organization headquartered in Washington, D.C., serves 2.2 million members and operates on an annual budget of almost $180 million. NEA's diversity initiatives include a meeting and convention protocol, which is overseen by the Equity and Ethnic Harmony Committee.

Before scheduling an annual meeting, NEA's convention staff meets with city officials, hotel managers, and the convention bureau. They address the following issues:

1. Are the city and site friendly to unions?
2. Does the site value diversity?
3. Is the site safe?
4. Is the site conveniently located, offering access to transportation, amusements, theaters, and family-oriented places and activities?
5. Can we negotiate a good price?

Before making a recommendation to NEA's board of directors, the convention manager presents the findings to the Minority Affairs Committee.

Making Flexible, Local Responses to Diversity

MARRIOTT INTERNATIONAL

Maintaining a flexible environment is a standard Marriott policy, says Sandy Leandro, senior diversity leader. For example, each property adapts its menus to the community it serves. Properties that serve international customers have multilingual sales representatives. Marriott's rooms can accommodate people with physical challenges, and some units have special phones, smoke alarms, and hookups to personal computers for the hearing impaired.

CHAPTER 4

USING COMMUNICATIONS TO DEMONSTRATE COMMITMENT

The organizations profiled in this book have recognized the need to address diversity in the messages they convey. They all use publications, marketing materials, and other image-building activities to reflect their commitment.

In their first wave of initiatives to improve communications, these organizations eliminated many thoughtless practices, such as pictures that didn't portray diversity, text and topics that offended some groups, exclusive use of the male pronoun, insensitive or overly complex writing, and unimaginative use of graphics and color. They also expanded their sensitivity beyond race and ethnicity to include gender, age, and other characteristics. Some designed their materials to meet the tastes and language preferences of different groups.

The most perceptive organizations have entered a second phase of communications management: demonstrating their commitment to diversity and explaining how that commitment translates into better products and customer service. These powerful messages are inextricably tied to the role of diversity in establishing competitive advantage in the marketplace.

To use communications in this manner, an organization must have successfully "walked the talk" of diversity. The following case study illustrates how one company uses an aggressive communications strategy to fan the flames of diversity.

CASE STUDY

AVON PRODUCTS, INC.

Spreading The Word About Diversity

Avon plans to be the premier company in providing opportunities for all people in all places where it conducts business. In pursuit of this goal, Avon focuses on recruiting the best people at every level, retaining associates by creating an environment where people accept differences and recognize individual contributions, and ensuring equity in advancement criteria. Simultaneously, Avon's leaders are busy spreading its vision: "To be the company that best understands and satisfies the product, service, and self-fulfillment needs of women globally."

Communications is critical in the diversity movement, according to Marcia L. Worthing, senior vice president of human resources. Not only can communications become a self-fulfilling prophecy for a corporation, she says, but it also "keeps the flame alive." Avon's early efforts, in the late 1970s and early 1980s, were primarily affirmative action strategies aimed at recruiting and retaining blacks and women. Today, the company is creating a culture that provides opportunities for all associates to reach their full potential in pursuit of corporate objectives. It's this new attitude that Avon's leaders continually talk about in person, in print, and on film.

Repeating the Message By Word of Mouth

Worthing says that diversity management is a positive, upbeat, humanistic approach to business. First and foremost, however, it's a key strategy for growth. Avon has based its diversity initiative on empowering employees worldwide, helping them develop respectful business relationships and form cross-functional teams, and distributing rewards for team and individual accomplishments.

To make sure the diversity effort remains an integral part of corporate life, Avon created a Diversity Council. The two vice presidents who co-chair the council are responsible for shaping the strategy on diversity and monitoring results. The director of diversity, who works closely with the council, is responsible for the business aspect of integrating diversity into the culture, systems, and practices.

Avon has made changes that directly benefit staff. For example, the company instituted a formal human resource review process that requires representatives from each country and department managers to discuss diversity issues and the employee mix in their areas. Five employee networks stage events and serve as a communications pipeline by bringing up issues important to constituents and by making suggestions.

Avon developed profiles for all professional positions; all the people who meet the requirements are offered an interview. Avon doesn't tolerate any disparagement of groups and expects its associates to comprehend and support the concept of valuing diversity. Leaders encourage mentoring of associates and require that performance appraisals include discussions of career development. For managers, performance appraisals address diversity efforts. They're rewarded for success in that area.

According to Worthing, managing diversity inside the corporation prepares Avon to manage it outside. For example, when soliciting requests for proposals from search firms, employment agencies, consultants, and universities, Avon asks for a description of the respondent's policy on diversity. The RFPs also ask for detailed information on the diversity of the team that would provide the services.

Avon incorporates diversity into the core curriculum of its educational programs, adds Al Smith, director of managing diversity. In the past, training consisted of one-day programs for senior officers. Now, training programs for senior managers address understanding differences, empowerment, and quality issues. Additionally, they learn about work engineering and fostering teamwork. In their training, sales representatives learn how to penetrate new markets and how different people have different needs. To associates, Avon reinforces the corporate outlook, what diversity means, and the business rationale for diversity.

Smith believes a company's flexibility contributes to competitive advantage. As a result, Avon offers 40 employee benefit programs, plus alternative work-arrangement (flex-time, telecommuting, job sharing), work and family, and elder-care programs. Company leaders remain sensitive to issues regarding lifestyles and workstyles, such as maternity leave and religious holidays.

Avon's community outreach efforts present additional opportunities to spread the word on diversity. Participants in the Black Executive Exchange Program speak to colleges about corporate America and Avon. An executive-loan program for nonprofit organizations does the same. Although minority vendors don't receive special concessions, Avon welcomes those that meet its quality standards. Its roster of suppliers has gone from 4 percent to 11 percent minority, and a national minority business association honored Avon as one of the leaders in minority vendor development.

Saying It Twice in Print

DIVERSITY: A Special Publication for Associates of Avon outlines the business of diversity for all to see. Peppered with testimonials and beliefs of people representing many groups, the publication serves as a teaching tool. In it, associates read about the different facets of diversity and how well the concept works at Avon. They learn about marketplace issues such as the diversity of Avon's models, support systems for Hispanic representatives and customers, a new cosmetic for women of dark complexion, efforts to serve African-American women, and programs for minority- and women-owned businesses. The range of workplace issues is equally broad, covering flexible scheduling, associate networks, gay rights, work redesign, leadership styles, sexual harassment, and coping with autoimmune deficiency syndrome (AIDS).

Avon also distributes publications on diversity to all associates and sales representatives. Its television and print advertisements incorporate diversity messages, and the company targets its marketing efforts to shared values, regardless of ethnic background or gender. Although 98 percent of Avon's sales are to women, staff say the male market also is important.

The *New York Times* (April 3, 1991) and the *Wall Street Journal* (April 4, 1994) helped spread the news to outsiders about how Avon does business on the inside. Both articles talked about the company's commitment to its sales representatives.

Saying It Thrice on Film

Jim Preston, Avon's chairman and chief executive officer, defines diversity as a source of competitive advantage. In a company video, he describes why affirmative action has outlived its usefulness in companies that are building a diverse workforce at all levels. He also highlights the seemingly small issues. For example, he says Avon once offered perks based on the lifestyles and preferences of its founders: a golf day, tickets to sports events, and trips to hunting and fishing lodges. Today, such perks may be perceived as symbols of exclusion.

Continuing Accomplishments

Avon is at the stage of transitioning from managing diversity to building an inclusive, high-performing organization. Diversity represents a key performance issue for line managers, who are responsible for integrating it with quality, reengineering, team-building, and empowerment initiatives. Functional departments—sales, marketing, and product development—have become cross-functional, multidisciplinary units.

Avon has shifted from a patriarchal management team to one that includes more women. Of 39 vice presidents, 15 are women—including the president, chief financial officer, general counsel, head of marketing, and head of sales.

Avon has no difficulty identifying and communicating the marketplace argument for diversity. Clearly, the capacity to win with diversity is necessary for success both in the corporate organization and the sales force. To understand and serve new markets—Vietnamese, Pakistani, Ghanaian, and Filipino women, for example—Avon needs managers and salespeople who can relate to people of difference.

PRACTICAL APPLICATIONS

In addition to ensuring that everyone understands the need for an integrated diversity initiative, communication strategies must publicize individuals' roles during implementation and the organization's ongoing commitment.

LESSONS LEARNED

- Successful organizations frame diversity and inclusiveness initiatives as integral parts of their standard operating procedures. Communications should reflect diversity in pictures and offend no group with the written word.
- Periodic communications are excellent tools for reminding staff, clients, and vendors of the organization's commitment.
- Organizations can take advantage of free publicity to showcase their efforts to build a diverse team and to participate in events honoring their commitment.
- It's easier to teach individual commitment to diversity when the organization's commitment is pervasive and fundamental to success.

That commitment should extend to all facets of company operations, including vendor relationships. Successful companies document their commitment and ask others to do the same.

- Organizations develop the capacity to effectively treat diversity in communications in several stages. The first stage involves consciousness raising and eliminating insensitive and inappropriate practices. The second stage involves segmenting publications to meet the needs of diverse groups. The third stage begins when the organization uses materials and image-building activities to communicate its diversity commitment in a more sophisticated manner.

HELPFUL HINTS

Getting Started

- **Make sure all existing documents are clear and nondiscriminatory.** Scrutinize publications to make sure they respect social, racial, and religious groups. Ensure that they reflect the range of diversity found in your industry, organization, and audience. Establish this review as standard operating procedure for all publishing staff.
- **Communicate with authors and other contributors.** Tell them of your efforts to combat discrimination and promote diversity in publications.
- **Locate vendors who can supply graphics and software that serve different market segments.** For example, don't assume all clip art is universally appealing. Go the extra mile to show diversity, even in simple drawings.
- **Publish diversity success stories.** For staff as well as customers, showcase what people are doing, where they're making progress, and what plans are in the works for making the organization truly inclusive. Encourage readers to respond.
- **Begin to segment and target communications efforts.** Develop competencies in understanding and serving different markets. Spread these skills broadly through the organization.
- **Develop a symbol of commitment.** Stage a contest to select the logo or slogan that best reflects your organization's commitment to diversity. Reproduce the winning entry on mugs, T-shirts, posters, and so forth.
- **Develop a library related to effective communications.** Appendix B includes recommended references.

Maintaining the Effort

- **Include diversity training as part of normal staff development.** Emphasize the marketplace link for diversity, communications, and image- building activities.
- **Give staff sufficient resources and authority to combat discrimination in all company documents.** Make certain that the CEO and other

managers understand that the publications staff must be empowered to do a first-class job.

- **Develop an editorial policy.** Publish a style manual and guide to producing communications. It should instruct authors on how to write inoffensively and list the most common traps to avoid.
- **Periodically have the publications staff talk about diversity with authors.** Two-way feedback is critical in improving performance: How well are authors writing for diverse audiences? How well does the publications staff communicate its needs?
- **Frequently solicit staff input.** Find out how the publications department can support the whole staff's growth and development.
- **Ensure your communications are well-received by a broad cross-section of readers.** Make reader preferences a key item in readership surveys.
- **Enlighten your readers about diversity and how it affects your industry, profession, or enterprise.** Instead of preaching, educate and provoke them to understand diversity and the marketplace argument for inclusiveness.
- **Use communications strategically.** Through your publications, communications, and image-building activities, position your organization as diverse, inclusive, and dedicated to customer service.

VIGNETTES

The following organizations we profiled have sophisticated ways of communicating their commitment to inclusiveness. These methods include advertisements and videos.

Feeling Like We Belong
WAL-MART

Wal-Mart, headquartered in Bentonville, Arkansas, has built partnerships with a collection of diverse businesses and vendors. In its advertising materials for Mothers Day 1994, Wal-Mart highlighted the role diversity plays in its operations.

The circular enabled the retailer to showcase diversity in terms of gender, ethnicity, age, and geography. In it children, spouses, and employees of the company and of associate firms modeled Wal-Mart's wares; also, proprietors of minority- and women-owned enterprises shared their personal stories and commented on their relationship with Wal-Mart.

Additionally, the featured suppliers confirmed their own and Wal-Mart's philosophy and commitments. Shared sentiments included growing a diverse workforce, supporting communities and charities, and achieving success despite the odds and naysayers. The ad featured Four Farmers in Miami, a supplier of fresh-cut flowers grown in Columbia; J.M. Products,

Inc., Little Rock; Luster Products, Inc., Chicago; and Soft Sheen, Chicago. Their message: Supporting their community members and organizations is part of their commitment "to give something back." The Cuban and Jewish co-founder of Dino Di Milano, Miami, and the proprietor of Designers Collection, Dallas, emphasized their keys to success: producing a quality product, taking risks, caring a lot about people, and being fair.

These are powerful messages. They proclaim the people at Wal-Mart are just like you and me. The models are real people, not mannequins, who say, "Wal-Mart respects and values all people."

Linking Minority Vendors and Corporations

National Minority Supplier Development Council (NMSDC)

A special section entitled "Minority Business Enterprises: Profit Through Partnership" in Fortune magazine (June 1994) shines the spotlight on the National Minority Supplier Development council (NMSDC). The section featured successful minority firms and those corporations that continue to make great strides in procuring products and services from minority vendors.

NMSDC, a national business membership organization, links minority business enterprises to more than 3,500 corporate members seeking services. The NMSDC Network includes a national office in New York and 42 regional offices. According to its president, Harriet R. Michel, NMSDC also helps corporate members develop, expand, and promote minority-purchasing programs. Certified minority businesses receive access to corporate members, technical assistance training, and support to grow their businesses and market their services.

NMSDC's corporate leaders unanimously agree on the value and wisdom of doing business with minority firms. Many have made significant commitments to minority sourcing. For example, Fortune reports that Chrysler, Ford, and General Motors purchased more than $2.5 billion in goods and services from minority suppliers in 1993. Their commitment to minority sourcing also extends to major suppliers, who the manufacturers ask to commit a percentage of their purchases to minority companies.

NMSDC, in fact, named Chrysler its "Corporation of the Year" for 1993, the year the auto maker spent nearly $750 million with minority-owned businesses. Chrysler required its biggest suppliers to commit the equivalent of 5 percent of their total sales to Chrysler to minority suppliers. The company also published a minority-supplier directory.

The goals, approaches, experiences, and programs of other NMSDC corporate members vary considerably. AT&T, for example, spawned its Minority and Women's Business Enterprise program in 1968. In 1993, the company purchased more than $780 million goods and services from minority- and women-owned businesses. Today, AT&T is expanding the role of these suppliers and subcontractors to make them significant partners in its strategic plan.

IBM's leaders, hoping that the small businesses they develop may become customers, have targeted minority suppliers since the early 1960s. In addition to spending more than $268 million with minority firms in 1993, IBM sponsored a three-day leadership seminar for minority business owners. The company also provides program managers and technical experts to assist the firms. As a participant in the "Rebuild Los Angeles" effort, for example, IBM pledged to create 300 jobs through local minority companies.

Another NMSDC corporate member, Northern Telecom, increased expenditures with minority- and women-owned businesses from 2.5 percent in 1980 to 11.8 percent in 1993. The company sponsors seminars for NMSDC-certified minority suppliers and provides supplier-diversity training for its buyers and employees. Another example of the variety of efforts is Xerox Corporation's mentoring program. The latest initiative of Xerox's Minority/Female Supplier Program teams minority firms with more established suppliers, who provide management and financial resources.

Presenting "Diversity: The Face of Hospitality"

AMERICAN HOTEL & MOTEL ASSOCIATION

The Diversity Task Force and Educational Institute of the American Hotel & Motel Association (AH&MA), Washington, D.C., created a video entitled "Diversity: The Face of Hospitality." The video prods lodging and hospitality professionals into thinking about how to manage a diverse workforce. Along with testimonials from hotel owners and operators, it presents managers with questions they can ask to assess their efforts. The video also describes the anticipated long- and short-term benefits of a well-managed diverse staff and ends with seven recommended steps for viewers to take.

Presenting "Racial and Cultural Bias in Medicine"

AMERICAN ACADEMY OF FAMILY PHYSICIANS

The American Academy of Family Physicians (AAFP), Kansas City, Missouri, addresses problems plaguing diverse medical staffs in its video "Racial and Cultural Bias in Medicine." Produced in 1991 by the academy's Committee on Minority Health Affairs, this video shows 27 dramatizations of blacks, Native Americans, and Hispanics facing racial or cultural bigotry in medical settings.

An accompanying guide is designed to stimulate discussion among physicians, residents, students, and teachers rather than to instruct them on how to resolve the situations. AAFP hopes the video will help sensitize viewers and reduce bias in medical situations.

Presenting "Culture: Alive and Well and Living in the Workplace"

NATIONAL ASSOCIATION FOR THE EDUCATION OF YOUNG CHILDREN

NAEYC's "Culture: Alive and Well and Living in the Workplace" represents the first step of the National Association for the Education of Young

Children to build awareness about diversity. The video records unrehearsed opinions of human service professionals as they define various components of culture and discuss the effects of stereotyping people and having unrealistic expectations. The interviewees also discuss the personal and professional dimensions of culture and the need to prepare children to deal with differences beyond the levels attained by their parents.

To deal with the issue of diversity in the workforce, on playgrounds, and with the association world, the film identifies three needs: training for teachers and families, developing change agents, and maintaining the momentum.

Presenting "Project Blueprint: A Plan for the Future"
UNITED WAY OF AMERICA

United Way of America (UWA), based in Alexandria, Virginia, developed "Project Blueprint: A Plan for the Future" to highlight the benefits of and strategies for developing culturally diverse volunteers. The video explores how cultural diversity training affects leadership and team building in local communities.

CHAPTER 5

INCREASING DIVERSITY WITHIN MEMBERSHIP ORGANIZATIONS

A membership organization faces two types of diversity challenges: one concerns its staff and the other its membership. Membership associations come about because people want to associate with others like themselves—they share a common interest, trade, profession, or cause. By their very nature, membership organizations are exclusive to some extent. As a result, building a diverse membership can pose a substantial challenge.

Although all members "own" their association's culture, a smaller group of leaders defines that culture. Obstacles to diversity may arise if these leaders lose touch with new trends and developments. Too, the "pipeline" of entry into the trade or profession may not offer equal access to people of difference. And it may take years for them to navigate the pipeline and qualify for membership. Therefore, increasing diversity proves somewhat more complicated for membership organizations than for corporations that must remain nimble and responsive to survive in the marketplace.

Yet powerful workforce and marketplace arguments exist for increasing the diversity of membership organizations. Given the composition of the current and future workforce, a trade or profession risks diminished capacity and power if it can't attract the best people from diverse groups. A professional or trade group with a homogeneous membership fails to prepare its members to compete with diverse organizations that are learning to win with diversity. Moreover, splinter groups based on difference will form if the association doesn't change to serve its diverse clientele.

In the first case study below, the American Association of University Women shares its diversity policy and sets an example for its chapters and affiliates to follow. The second case study illustrates how the Society for Human Resource Management offers its members a model that they can translate into their own settings.

CASE STUDY

AMERICAN ASSOCIATION OF UNIVERSITY WOMEN

Embracing Diversity to Redefine the Organization

The American Association of University Women (AAUW), headquartered in Washington, D.C., advocates educational equity for women and girls. In the late 1980s, its leaders began examining the organization's mission and composition with the aim of reversing a decline in membership.

Through focus groups, AAUW determined that women of color, women with disabilities, and women of different sexual orientation were interested in its mission but weren't joining.

With the help of consultants, trainers, and the board of directors, AAUW made changes that had significant effects:

- In 1987 AAUW opened its membership to men.
- It launched a publicity campaign, which increased to 30 percent the total applications and awards made to women of color.
- AAUW redefined a fellowship program targeted to women of color.
- The association forged links with groups such as the National Council of Negro Women; ASPIRA Association, Inc.; and numerous Hispanic, Pan-Asian, and women's education caucuses.

AAUW has since invested in a series of program, training, and visibility initiatives, sponsoring more than 100 diversity workshops between 1990 and 1993. Membership has grown to 150,000. In the process, AAUW has become a multicultural organization both inside and out. In fact, AAUW used to hire models so its publications would appeal to a broader clientele; now its real members illustrate the organization's multiculturalism.

To help its 51 state and 1,750 local branches become multicultural as well, AAUW sets an example and standards for them to follow. For example, the national headquarters sponsors a five-star competition through which branches can win grants or prizes: One star represents diversity. Another major strategy to increase membership diversity involves AAUW's participation in coalitions; this activity both broadens its knowledge of diverse cultures and extends its reach into the broader community. AAUW also sponsors mentoring programs and math/science days for girls in diverse communities.

Becoming a Model Multicultural Organization

The changes in marketing strategy and organizational objectives affected AAUW from the national level to individual members. To ensure they practice what they preach—and serve as a model to branches—AAUW's leaders and staff are involved in a number of diversity efforts.

Anne L. Bryant, AAUW's executive director, identifies two prerequisites to becoming a multicultural organization. First, she says, the organization needs a team approach to leadership. Second, everyone must believe that becoming a multicultural organization carries the same importance as any other goal in the association's strategic plan.

In the article "Creating a Multicultural Association" (*Leadership*, 1991), Bryant shares the steps that leaders and staff can take to change an organization. The steps include the following:

- Gain commitment from the top.
- Understand what becoming a multicultural organization really means.

- Understand how to work in cooperation with people from diverse backgrounds.
- Experience diversity through training on how to build coalitions.
- Establish concrete, measurable, and doable goals early on.
- Undertake parallel efforts at all staff levels.
- Work with coalitions of diverse groups.

As a result of these efforts, Bryant says, AAUW has made great strides in recruiting and promoting a diverse staff. Leaders not only recruit non-traditional employees for high-level positions but also fill entry-level positions with a diversity of white employees. The staff of 90 includes Asian Americans/Pacific Islanders, Hispanics, African Americans, and European Americans—as well as males and females, gays and lesbians, and young and mature people.

Maintaining this multicultural environment takes considerable effort. Employees receive diversity training annually, and one staff working group deals with internal cultural issues. The group, for instance, ensures that various faiths are highlighted during holidays so no one feels excluded.

AAUW uses principles of Total Quality Management (TQM) and self-managed work teams as focal points for staff development. The staff empowerment council has 10 members who represent all levels within the organization, most of the departments, and major function areas. The council is racially and sexually diverse. Another group, the Diversity Consultant Corps, is composed of 10 volunteer members. The corps advises AAUW on the steps it must take to become a model of a multicultural organization.

Publicizing the Commitment

AAUW leaders found that communicating the association's commitment is an integral part of maintaining their diversity efforts. For starters, all publications, program materials, membership recruitment kits, and foundation fellowship applications must include the full diversity statement: *"In principle and in practice, the American Association of University Women (AAUW) values and seeks a diverse membership. There shall be no barriers to full participation in this organization on the basis of gender, race, creed, age, sexual orientation, national origin, or disability."*

AAUW has willingly shared its secrets of success with the wider association community. In addition to writing an article on AAUW's diversity policy and strategies for a trade magazine, Bryant serves as co-chair of the task force on diversity appointed by the Greater Washington Society of Association Executives. She requested that an African-American male association executive serve as the co-chair.

Ensuring That No One Feels Excluded

AAUW focuses its diversity efforts on staff training, organizational change, and the development and distribution of products and services.

In addition, Bryant notes, it's important that no one feels excluded at AAUW's meetings. That might mean taking advantage of technological advances such as closed-captioned projections, better sound systems, and large screens for the deaf and visually impaired. When evaluating a potential site, AAUW's convention manager scrutinizes whether it's truly friendly to people in wheelchairs, with seeing-eye dogs, or with other physical challenges.

Bryant believes the staff have become sensitive to differences and learned to take a broad perspective when deciding where to host meetings, what food to serve, which speakers to invite, and how to design the agenda. At meetings, AAUW appoints someone to pay attention to newcomers and make them feel comfortable. The bottom line, says Bryant, is that meetings must show that the hosting organization is sensitive to the needs of others.

All the components of AAUW's commitment to diversity inter-relate. Its efforts to invite diverse members and employees relate to its goal of creating a comfortable environment for working and meeting. In turn, these efforts provide the materials for communicating the association's intent and experiences.

CASE STUDY

SOCIETY FOR HUMAN RESOURCE MANAGEMENT
Advancing Understanding of Diversity

For many years the Society for Human Resource Management (SHRM), Alexandria, Virginia, has served as educator, resource, and legislative liaison for its members—60,000 human resource managers. Since 1992, its staff of 90 has worked on bringing the concept of diversity to both its internal and external publics. Responding to a challenge from its top elected leader, SHRM made a commitment to fostering a climate of inclusiveness. Its plan included the following steps:

- Conduct a survey of the human resource field to determine who is doing what in terms of defining and implementing diversity programs.
- Include diversity goals in the strategic plan. (This included obtaining diverse representation of members, staff, and board members.)
- Educate, train, and develop staff in the area of diversity.
- Develop resources to help educate members and organizations in general.
- Participate in consciousness-raising activities.

SHRM's diversity initiative has yielded concrete results on all five points. The results of the survey, published and disseminated in 1993, provided members with an overview of diversity efforts and issues facing human resource personnel. SHRM incorporated diversity goals into its strategic plan not as a "diversity block" but as specified numbers and targets interspersed throughout the plan.

SHRM's primary goal is to influence its members, making them active partners in the effort to foster an inclusive culture on local, national, and international levels. The society sets an example and expects a trickle-down effect throughout its membership. More specifically, SHRM helps its leaders, staff, and members address workforce issues of diversity through meeting planning, resource and program development, and communications activities.

Making Meetings Work

SHRM has developed a diversity track for its annual and international conferences. In developing a conference agenda, meeting planners not only look at functional areas in the human resource profession but also focus on different aspects of the diversity issue. SHRM requires keynote speakers to reflect the organization's commitment in their remarks.

Planning relevant and enlightening sessions isn't an option but a necessity, explains Grace Prindle, manager of international and diversity programs. SHRM also makes an effort to ensure that meetings are comfortable for everyone. Most of SHRM's activities attract American attendees and focus on domestic concerns. The annual conference, however, provides a special opportunity to serve international guests. Attendees from outside the United States receive a full orientation, welcome, and preview of the conference, plus friendship pins showing their country's flag and the U.S. flag. To facilitate the participation of Spanish-speaking guests, the society provides simultaneous interpretation.

Developing Resources

Conducting meetings represents only one way SHRM keeps its members up to date. Staff are building a resource network for members who want to learn about initiating diversity programs, foster a more inclusive culture in their environment, or simply contact "people in the know." Also in development is a database practitioners can access to find out who is doing what. The names of training consultants as well as members willing to serve as resources appear in the database—which members can also use as a networking tool.

To help its members avoid reinventing the wheel, SHRM recently undertook a benchmarking activity. The society surveyed the field, identified successful diversity programs, and published its "best practice" findings.

Communicating on Multiple Fronts

In membership publications—*HR News* and *HR Magazine*—and in the staff newsletter *From Our Corner*, SHRM leaders reiterate the importance of addressing diversity. For example, each issue of *HR News* features a story about diversity; the monthly magazine devotes a column to the topic.

In addition, SHRM silently broadcasts its commitment with a "diversity pin." Initially designed to be worn as a symbolic gesture of SHRM's commitment, the pin has since become a hot-selling item to nonmembers and other organizations.

Preparing for Tomorrow

SHRM simply listens to its members and gives them what they want—education and direction, says Grace Prindle. This involves planning meetings, creating resources, and sharing communications. But, she says, these methods and tools do more than simply remind members of SHRM's commitment to diversity: They also bolster the society's mission to broaden its members' experiences by exposing them to current practices and leading-edge technologies.

PRACTICAL APPLICATIONS

Given the large number of organizations around today, people can afford to be picky. Membership organizations must make the effort to have accurate profiles of their members and to serve them effectively.

LESSONS LEARNED

- Attracting a diverse membership often means changing the organizational culture to become more comfortable and welcoming. New members like to see themselves represented in staff and membership positions.
- When bringing together people from different cultures, organizations become most effective by creating a new culture that's an amalgamation. Accepting a predominant culture from one of the groups repeats the sins of the past.
- The organizations that are winning with diversity have found that the marketplace argument for diversity and inclusiveness is the most powerful instrument for continual, pervasive organizational change and adaptation.
- Potential members from diverse backgrounds may have many reasons for not joining your organization. Perhaps competing organizations currently meet their needs better, or maybe they've had unpleasant experiences with your organization. Another possibility: Your organization has failed to communicate that its portfolio of products can meet their needs.
- An association attempting to attract a diverse membership must set the example in its staff. (See Chapter 6 for information on how to build commitment from a diverse workforce.)

HELPFUL HINTS

Getting Started

- **Gain commitment from the volunteer leaders and CEO.** Without such commitment at the outset, your efforts to increase the diversity of membership won't succeed.
- **Understand what is meant by building a diverse and inclusive membership.** In addition to diversifying staff and membership, an inclusive organization accepts responsibility for laying the pipeline for the future. Study the requirements and benefits of becoming an inclusive organization; learn about the barriers and pitfalls.
- **Analyze what diverse members would want from your association.** Ask potential members what they want and need from associations, how many of those needs are being answered, and who is answering them. This requires focus group work and sophisticated market research.
- **Assess your association's attractiveness to a diverse membership.** Review your membership materials, publications, meetings and conferences, and other communications and image-building activities. What face does your organization put forward? Corrective actions may be in order.
- **Have staff and volunteer leaders participate in diversity training.** They should learn what a diverse membership needs and how your association's offerings appeal to a diverse membership. Focus on what diversity means and how it relates to your organization's purpose and bottom line.
- **Open lines of communication between members and leaders.** Enable all levels to share ideas, determine reachable goals, and make plans to change discriminatory practices or policies.
- **Develop a mailing list of minority organizations in your industry or profession.** Make contact with your counterparts and start sharing information.
- **Conduct an informal survey of staff and membership.** Get a feel for how people perceive diversity issues and interpret your organization's activities. This will help you gauge efforts and determine whether to consult specialists.
- **Determine novel ways to emphasize the CEO's commitment to diversity.** All staff and members must know this commitment translates into all facets of the organization's operation.
- **Stage a "Proud to be Diverse" contest.** Ask members to send in their ideas for addressing diversity in and through the organization.

Maintaining the Effort

- **Establish goals for corrective actions and measurable outcomes.** Identify which products, services, and participation opportunities you must refashion to attract a diverse range of people. Set goals and milestones for increasing diverse membership.
- **Establish coalitions and working partnerships with other groups.** If minority-focused associations exist within your trade, profession, or philanthropy, get on good terms with them. On some matters you may be competitors—in many more areas you'll be collaborators.
- **Incorporate diversity and inclusiveness into your strategic plan.** Do not block the components into a separate initiative. Rather, weave elements of diversity throughout the plan.
- **Become a leader in the industry or profession.** Once your organization makes the commitment to valuing diversity, determine how you can provide leadership and serve as a resource to members. Include this goal in your diversity plan.
- **Hold members accountable for diversity-related goals.** Develop rewards for compliance with policies and initiatives—and develop consequences for any failure to comply.
- **Work on integrating the diversity effort into all member communications.** Solicit feedback and share successes regularly.
- **Showcase your organization's commitment at meetings and events.** Make sure diverse groups are visibly represented in all levels and are made to feel welcome.
- **Institute strategies to remove barriers to success.** Training programs and mentor relationships are two ways to help underrepresented groups gain experience.
- **Evaluate and document internal and external gains.** Periodically evaluate everyone's progress in achieving diversity goals. This can serve as a morale booster— "See how far we've come." When little progress has occurred, periodic evaluations help everyone get back on track.
- **Give all groups a voice in governance.** It makes little sense to encourage groups to help orchestrate positive and productive change and then not give them a role in the governance.
- **Enlist the help of schools and organizations that provide members.** Inform sources of potential recruits about your diversity efforts, and encourage them to participate.
- **Keep the lines of communication open.** Use contact people, periodicals, and bulletin boards. Give members a means to voice concerns, air grievances, provide feedback, and share ideas regularly.
- **Expand your diversity reference library.** See Appendix B for recommendations.

The following associations have tailored their approaches to increasing diversity to the unique characteristics of their memberships.

Accelerating the Careers of Diverse Executives

AMERICAN SOCIETY OF ASSOCIATION EXECUTIVES

In 1989, the American Society of Association Executives (ASAE), Washington, D.C., formed its Committee on Diversity in Association Management. Since then the committee has launched several initiatives to increase the involvement of people of color in association management.

One program concentrates on accelerating the careers of diverse groups of association executives. The program works like this: Chief executives nominate people of color within their staffs who have at least two years' work experience in the association field. From this group ASAE's Diversity Committee selects candidates to receive a free ASAE membership. For one year, the recipients can attend ASAE education programs and conventions for free and participate in networking opportunities with peers. Finally, they're matched with mentors to assist in their career planning.

Two years into the program, ASAE increased the likelihood of making successful mentoring matches. Candidates now request the race or ethnicity, expertise, and gender of their mentors. Other program changes include requiring mentors and proteges to attend training sessions and providing more structured meetings. The mentors benefit from these relationships as well, says Debra Sher, vice president of the member services division—they learn how to recruit and hire executives of color for their own organizations.

ASAE committees and councils now have at least two ethnic or racial minority members, and all conventions include at least one session on the issue of diversity. Marketing materials reflect faces of color, and each year several issues of *Association Management*, ASAE's monthly magazine, address the topic of diversity. Recently the ASAE board approved changes in the "Standards of Conduct" for association executives. By joining the society, members agree that they "refuse to engage in, or countenance, discrimination on the basis of race, sex, age, religion, national origin, sexual orientation, or disability."

Using Constituency Groups to Address Issues

AMERICAN ACADEMY OF FAMILY PHYSICIANS

The American Academy of Family Physicians (AAFP), a national organization headquartered in Kansas City, Missouri, has a $45 million annual budget and diverse staff of 260. When AAFP leaders realized its membership of 79,000 didn't reflect the female and nonwhite physician population, they created three constituency groups to address age, gender, and race issues.

Over the past few years, groups for new physicians, women in family medicine, and minority physicians have helped AAFP make significant progress toward its goal of balanced representation. These groups hold special events at the AAFP annual meeting; conduct networking and training activities; and publicize their findings and concerns through annual reports, white papers, and audiovisual presentations.

Their latest and most powerful activity includes participating in governance of the academy. Recently the three groups combined their meetings with AAFP's annual leadership meeting, which gave them greater visibility and access to board members. AAFP changed its bylaws to grant all three constituency groups the ability to send resolutions to the annual conference. The groups elect and send voting delegates to the AAFP Congress as well.

Increasing Sensitivity and Understanding

NATIONAL ASSOCIATION OF PURCHASING MANAGEMENT

The National Association of Purchasing Management (NAPM), Tempe, Arizona, has more than 36,000 members in 178 affiliates across the United States and Puerto Rico. In 1991 NAPM's board of directors appointed an ad hoc committee to investigate minority involvement in the association and the profession. When the committee presented its results, it proposed a plan of action to interject diversity throughout all levels of NAPM. The committee emphasized that NAPM needed to further sensitize itself and its members and to actively integrate diversity within the organization's policies, programs, and publications.

Within three months of the proposal's approval, NAPM conducted training for the board and staff to increase their sensitivity to and understanding of diversity. NAPM continually works to create an open, flexible, and responsive environment for members. For example, the association encourages minorities to fill volunteer leadership roles and staff positions. In addition to addressing general issues and concerns in its monthly magazine, NAPM seeks out authors from diverse backgrounds and makes an effort to use photographs and artwork depicting diversity.

NAPM included the following statement in its 1994-95 strategic plan:

> In principle and practice, the National Association of Purchasing Management values and seeks a diverse membership. Individual viewpoints and contributions are pursued and respected. There are no barriers to full participation in NAPM on the basis of ethnic background, gender, creed, age, sexual orientation, national origin, or disability.

For NAPM, diversity is valuing and respecting individual strengths, viewpoints, and contributions. Diversity is viewed as a positive asset in NAPM's growth and success. The association will value and embrace diversity in the membership.

NAPM values the effort, knowledge, and commitment of all volunteers and staff, and structures the volunteer system to maintain continuity by encouraging participation in integrated activities to eliminate waste and duplication.

Taking a Tailored Approach

AMERICAN HOTEL & MOTEL ASSOCIATION

For its 12,000 members, the Washington, D.C.-based American Hotel & Motel Association (AH&MA) provides education, resources, information, and lobbying. It also serves as spokesperson for a membership that includes vendors, property owners, international associates, faculty, and students. Complaints from two groups prompted the association to respond as both a learner and leader: Asian-American constituents felt "segmented," and operators of economy lodgings felt "outside of the mainstream."

Because many of its members also belong to the Asian American Hotel Owners Association (AAHOA), AH&MA now participates in AAHOA activities, exhibits at its conventions, and mails information on state activities to its members. In addition, AH&MA appointed a task force to explore ways in which the two organizations can work together. These endeavors give AH&MA visibility and show Asian members that AH&MA cares about their community and their concerns.

AH&MA currently dedicates one of its meetings to addressing the needs of economy-lodging operators. To help the membership at large, the association produced a teaching video entitled "Diversity: The Face of Hospitality" and sends speakers to state-level affairs.

Making Certain Leaders and Staff "Get It"

AMERICAN LUNG ASSOCIATION/AMERICAN THORACIC SOCIETY (ALA/ATS)

For cultural diversity to thrive within the American Lung Association/ American Thoracic Society (ALA/ATS), which encompasses 115 separately incorporated lung associations and a national staff of 190, a two-tiered approach is necessary. First, association administrators seek culturally diverse and educated volunteers, staff, and board members. Second, employees at the New York City headquarters receive diversity training, which a manager of cultural diversity and a consultant oversee.

Recently, ALA's 27-member national board approved a five-point plan to help members implement the association's cultural diversity initiative. The document contains facts on diversity as well as strategies and timelines for:

1. Developing staffs and boards that reflect the ethnic and cultural mix of the community.
2. Ensuring that programs, activities, and communications are designed appropriately and are culturally sensitive.
3. Supporting nontraditional scientists and researchers.

4. Encouraging research in minority health issues.

5. Increasing the use of minority vendors.

Diversifying Membership in a Low-Key Manner

ASSOCIATION OF AMERICAN RAILROADS (AAR)

The Association of American Railroads (AAR), Washington, D.C., decided to take a "low-key and quiet approach" to diversifying its membership. The result? AAR members have found a number of opportunities for collaboration and have avoided negative responses.

A committee comprised of diversity practitioners in the industry meets several times a year to discuss EEO compliance issues, Americans with Disabilities Act (ADA) accommodations, and other legislative issues. This is critical to the association's mission to monitor legislation and keep members informed. Additionally, staff members meet quarterly with the chief executive officer to report on new diversity initiatives and resources.

Lastly, AAR is addressing the underrepresentation of minorities and women in the engineering ranks of research and testing departments. It has developed networks at universities to identify and groom student interns for possible future employment. The association plans to expand the program to other parts of the organization, while continuing to serve as a role model nationwide.

Mainstreaming Diversity into All Activities

INTERNATIONAL ASSOCIATION OF BUSINESS COMMUNICATORS

Once its U.S. members alerted the chairman to the problems minorities face in the field and in the association, the International Association of Business Communicators (IABC), San Francisco, established a task force. IABC formalized its attempts to address diversity by turning the task force into its Multiculturalism Committee, which focuses on issues affecting blacks, Hispanics, and Asians.

Although members primarily drove the diversity movement, IABC's leaders added the perspective that communicators must understand their jobs from an international perspective. They also wanted members to become attuned to conflict resolution and negotiation, which often are issues of culture. For IABC, educating members to become more effective in their jobs means addressing issues that go beyond race and ethnicity.

Just as association leaders came to believe that diversity and communication issues are inseparable, they concluded an appreciation of cultural differences was needed as well. Culture equals common and shared values, attitudes, and beliefs that shape behavior. IABC aims to foster communication excellence through an understanding of human diversity, the dimensions of which include race, ethnicity, color, creed, religion, physical ability, gender, sexual orientation, age, national origin, and language.

IABC promotes this understanding internally and within the profession by:

- Increasing and supporting diversity with IABC membership.
- Heightening awareness and understanding of diversity among leaders and members.
- Developing a body of knowledge regarding multiculturalism in the workplace and marketplace in each country where IABC has chapters. This involves researching trends and issues in multiculturalism and diversity as they apply to organizational communication.
- Increasing awareness of IABC's leadership and activity in multiculturalism within the communication and business communities.

The Multiculturalism Committee attempts to mainstream all association activities into the concept of diversity. For example, every board member has the charge of examining the relevance of diversity in the organization. At speaking engagements, the chief executive and senior officers always underscore IABC's commitment to diversity and its importance to the communication profession.

Elizabeth Allan, IABC's senior vice president, has seen awareness and understanding increase among members and leaders. More people now attend conference sessions on diversity, and the composition of the board and conference speakers has changed. The 1994 conference included a session on sexual orientation and the communication profession, and speakers from various countries addressed conflict resolution from a cultural perspective. An advisory committee chooses the conference's content and speakers with an eye toward representing the membership's geographic and professional differences.

But IABC isn't stopping there. It has in the works a "train the trainer" program; a kit to help chapters develop diversity programs; and a bibliography of resources, speakers, and consultants. It also plans to conduct research in all countries with IABC chapters, with the goal of developing a body of knowledge that makes diversity relevant to each locale. Allan believes the best measurement of IABC's success is the degree to which its leaders have incorporated diversity concerns into decisions regarding budgets, programming, and board assignments.

Launching a New Diversity Initiative
INTERNATIONAL ASSOCIATION OF FIRE CHIEFS

Headquartered in Fairfax, Virginia, the International Association of Fire Chiefs (IAFC) has a staff of 25 and an annual budget of $3.1 million. This association recently made a commitment to setting an example for its 10,000 members, enabling them to make changes and implement diversity awareness training in their departments.

The headquarters staff first formed a five-member task force to help make employees cognizant of cultural issues. Next, IAFC formed a 10-member national task force, which examined the membership and field to determine ways to recruit diverse employees at the local level. The first recommendation: Include the phrase "women and minorities encouraged to apply" on all fire department applications.

The association has added a diversity session to its annual conference and initiated a relationship with the Black Professional Fire Fighters Association. Fire chiefs can use a "hotline" to call the IAFC executive director to discuss sensitive issues and to obtain advice.

Serving Diverse and International Members

INTERNATIONAL SLEEP PRODUCTS ASSOCIATION

The International Sleep Products Association (ISPA), Alexandria, Virginia, represents approximately 600 companies. These range from mom-and-pop stores to Fortune 500 corporations. Other differences include franchisors and franchisees and members from 60 countries and many regions; the association also has a strong Jewish contingent.

ISPA welcomes such diversity because it "can't represent the trade unless there's a place for everyone who lives off the trade," says Russell L. Abolt, executive vice president. Although ISPA has never specifically addressed racial and social integration issues, it values its constituents' diversity by emphasizing individual skill development and potential for advancement.

"When an organization is ambitious and has strong goals for itself and its constituency, it digs for the best everyone has to offer and then focuses on strengths rather than on weaknesses," says Abolt. The result, he adds, is that the institution also becomes a tool for personal growth and development.

ISPA has a committee of international business and has found little need to make special accommodations for the varied constituents. However, it offers translation at some meetings. International suppliers have launched their own newsletters and have become involved in developing programs for ISPA conferences.

CHAPTER 6

BUILDING COMMITMENT FROM A DIVERSE WORKFORCE

O rganizations in the managing diversity stage—those using diversity to establish competitive advantage—find their efforts require a new form of social contract. The organization demonstrates its commitment to systematically removing barriers to performance, evaluating employees solely on their capacity to understand and meet customers' needs. It agrees to empower its employees to solve problems and to shape the culture. In return, employees agree to meet the needs of customers in the face of fierce competition and to perform to world-class standards. Both the organization and individual employees hold one another to high standards of performance, which are effectively communicated and well understood. And both sides cooperate in developing a flexible, responsive organizational culture.

The following case study portrays the efforts of Ortho Biotech, Inc., a subsidiary of Johnson & Johnson, to create a high-performing culture with expectations of world-class performance.

CASE STUDY

ORTHO BIOTECH, INC.

Creating Shared Values and a Distinctive Culture

In 1990 Ortho Biotech, Inc. (OBI), a division of the Pharmaceutical Company, became a separate operating company. Facing stiff marketplace challenges and wishing to part with its parent company's traditional culture, OBI decided to break new ground.

Following a cultural audit at its parent company, OBI's newly appointed board and president participated in diversity awareness training. They learned how racist and sexist attitudes and behaviors were embedded in American corporate culture and recognized the need for a radically different culture. When developing a strategic plan, OBI's leaders chose to make valuing diversity as important an objective as strengthening teamwork, enhancing creativity and innovation, and encouraging participative management. They considered these principal elements essential to creating a "flat, lean machine"—one not steeped in tradition but capable of navigating the competitive challenges of the 1990s.

Laying the Foundation

Leaving nothing to chance, OBI created the Managing Diversity Task Force. Its goal was to develop standards on which to build a new corporate culture, one that valued individual and group differences and fostered effective management of all employees. A year later, its goal accomplished, the task force expanded to include board members and became the Culture Development Committee. This was a critical move for keeping alive the effort to integrate diversity initiatives with OBI's business mission.

The new committee's goals included modeling and monitoring behavioral norms that would support, acknowledge, and appreciate the differences of race and gender. With the assistance of an external consultant, the committee developed a series of workshops called "Adventures in Cultural Enhancement." The workshops permitted all OBI employees to challenge, change, or uphold the corporate vision statement as well as the norms and behaviors developed by the committee. Workshop leaders also taught skills for working in the new culture and for developing plans to move the culture toward the corporate vision.

Affinity groups comprised of people with similar concerns emerged from these workshops. The affinity groups met to support members, identify concerns, and determine and recommend appropriate actions. In addition, OBI formed task teams to carry out specific tasks associated with the culture development effort.

This initial effort to develop and introduce the OBI corporate culture took approximately two years. The Culture Development Committee then took on a new identify—the Energy Source. The group's goal was to empower the affinity groups and task teams. Its first actions included establishing a decision-making model for reviewing proposals submitted by the groups and teams and developing a strategy to fund the approved proposals. Within three months the African-American Affinity Group had presented its findings. The other groups and task teams submitted mission statements and identified operational problems. Board members worked with various subcommittee members to address the issues raised. One subset of the Energy Source—the Culture Steering Committee—guided the overall culture-setting effort. Chaired by a board member, the committee had diverse members who represented every OBI division.

The culture-development process started with committed leaders. Next, groups representing diverse people, structures, and processes worked to extend the corporate vision throughout the company. Only then could leaders start building staff commitment to and enthusiasm for the new culture.

Building Staff Commitment

OBI leaders contend that inclusive staffs don't just happen. A company must build a common culture with deliberate effort and sustain it through continued and focused attention. OBI's president, Dennis Longstreet, outlines the steps to take: Develop a statement of shared vision, articulate how to reach the vision, identify and address obstacles, and maintain the momentum.

In a recent interview (*The Executive Direction*, January 1994),

Longstreet explained that all of OBI's employees participated in developing the corporate vision statement. Today each carries the corporate vision on a laminated card. Because they collaborated in its development, employees "own" the statement and therefore have a commitment to accomplishing it. OBI also found employee participation critical for the development of behavioral norms. Although OBI's commitment to ensuring an inclusive workforce requires proactive employee participation, Longstreet contends that the company creates, develops, and models an inclusive corporate culture.

OBI paid particular attention to building awareness. Workshops held in 1992 and 1993 focused on acknowledging that racism and sexism exist at OBI, showing how diversity plays out in the OBI culture, and teaching skills necessary to work in the new OBI culture. Now employee workshops explore differences of all kinds and teach respect for those differences.

The term "differences" encompasses characteristics identified by employees. OBI doesn't treat differences as a basis for entitlement or special recognition, nor is one difference superior to another. OBI expects everyone to display understanding, commit to the shared vision, and— more important—exhibit behavior that supports OBI's daily business practices. Finally, employees both individually and collectively make a commitment to excelling in the marketplace.

The people who helped develop OBI's culture say the key components of building an inclusive staff are identifying and addressing obstacles. Problems, they say, are inevitable and should be addressed before becoming large enough to detract from the corporate goal. For example, early on the committees, task forces, and affinity groups addressed the following issues:

- At start up, the Managing Diversity Task Force members had little board-level guidance and no evaluation process to gauge their effectiveness. They found that white women and people of color weren't likely to lead diversity efforts because white men held the greatest power in the organization and maintained the status quo.
- The Culture Development Committee had difficulty defining criteria for assessment, setting timelines for the completion of intermediate steps, and justifying the costs in employee time and corporate expenses.
- Middle-level managers questioned the fairness of having to acquire skills to succeed in an emerging culture while still being held accountable to rules that hadn't yet changed.

OBI leaders responded by developing policies that required all committees, teams, and groups to be heterogeneous (across race, gender, and job level). They modified accountability standards to accommodate the difficulties in measuring progress and success in the culture-development effort. And they acknowledged managers' concerns. There was no denying that some employees, notably white male managers, felt they lost certain privileges. Nonetheless, the managers, too, formed an affinity group to engender support.

Affinity groups not only provide members with a support structure but also address the obstacles confronting OBI's change agents, says Andrea Zintz, vice president for human resources. Affinity groups raise issues relevant to cultural change and behavior, often proposing structural and system-wide changes for the board to act on. Granted, not all problems have an immediate solution, yet OBI leaders believe in identifying and addressing the problems in some manner. "We try to create a safe environment to allow everyone's potential for creative energy and power to bubble up," says Zintz.

Meetings at OBI provide a forum for leaders to listen and an opportunity for the company to show its commitment by example. Keeping attendees' comfort in mind, planners set up the room to encourage audience participation and require presenters to engage the audience rather than remain at the podium.

In its founding stages, OBI disavowed traditional standards for speech, appearance, and opinions that block a person's access to higher levels. Leaders continue to disregard superficial factors that create differences and focus on staff contributions. They also look for candidates who can flourish in OBI's culture; in other words, people who denigrate others need not apply. These ongoing efforts help OBI maintain its momentum in fostering diversity. The company continues to create work teams along heterogeneous lines and requires both board and staff members to receive training in how to manage diverse cultures. Managers receive rewards for diversifying—and penalties if they don't.

OBI hasn't limited its commitment to diversity to just increasing the numbers of nonwhite males in its executive ranks. Its leaders also want visible and tangible evidence that the philosophy of creating an inclusive workforce is working.

Getting Help From the Board

OBI includes everyone in diversity awareness training. More important, the company tailors the training to the group's needs. For example, OBI leaders learn how to behave in company meetings. Board members are instructed not to cluster together when they attend functions; they're encouraged to participate in, but not dominate, discussions, conversations, and presentations.

Clearly this represents a step beyond simply changing the board's composition to reflect diversity. It enables employees to see leaders engaging in the same behaviors they're held accountable for.

Reaping the Benefits

Developing and implementing a new culture yields learning opportunities and benefits for everyone, observes Dennis Longstreet. OBI leaders have tuned into listening and responding to employees, and the new culture encourages all employees to voice their concerns.

OBI wouldn't be a leader in the biopharmaceutical market had its leaders ignored employee concerns voiced during the parent company's cultural audit. They heard employees' complaints of inequities, indignities, and the inability to contribute. These findings, in fact, made managing diversity a top priority. Now affinity group members willingly voice their concerns, knowing management will listen and respond. Longstreet, who meets regularly with affinity groups, has said, "This isn't about designing a customized approach for every group and every issue. It's about listening to people—their problems and their aspirations."

OBI meeting professionals listen as well. Through focus groups and surveys, they find out what participants want and then deliver. This has resulted in scheduling dates to avoid religious holidays, softening the application of traditional dress codes, devising alternate activities, and modifying the length of seminars. Zintz believes the dynamic, responsive meetings at OBI are a product of listening—and valuing what's heard.

Adopting a Good Business Practice

The stiff marketplace competition doesn't bother Zintz: "Because we can turn on a dime, we can respond to change," she says. Simply put, OBI isn't steeped in tradition, so cultural change comes easier. The smallness and tightness of operations cannot tolerate any barriers that would stifle employee creativity.

The leaders have also learned to keep moving so the company doesn't become static—they constantly reinvent the culture. For example, to ensure the cultural-developmental process remains tied to corporate practices and policies, they study how performance reviews, job descriptions, and expectations relate to the management of a diverse organization.

Having made the commitment to a diverse workforce, OBI's leaders and staff enjoy many benefits, including high performance, fast turnaround, high productivity, high morale, and increased employee motivation. Reports indicate sales have increased 50 percent, and employee turnover stands at about 8 percent. OBI gives its employees a stake in developing and maintaining an environment in which they can thrive. The company's reward is a committed staff that works to prevent standard corporate "isms"—racism, sexism, ageism—from invading the carefully crafted environment.

Three characteristics place OBI ahead of most other biopharmaceutical firms and many corporations: leadership's commitment to creating an inclusive culture, organizational structures that support the philosophy, and a participative workforce.

Practical Applications

Each organization should establish a formal structure for implementing diversity initiatives. Involve those who'll be accountable for developing staff roles and responsibilities. Leaders of meeting and hospitality enterprises must vocalize their commitment to an inclusive work environment and illustrate how such a commitment satisfies both employees and customers.

Lessons Learned

- Diversity means more than racial and gender differences. Define diversity in broad terms, and focus on eliminating barriers to successful performance and advancement for all people.
- Diversity management is first and foremost a key business strategy for growth.
- Employees must understand the corporate outlook, what diversity means, and the business rationale for diversity.
- In the early stages, earmark resources specifically for diversity efforts.
- All employees must participate in developing a work environment they'll be enthusiastic about and committed to supporting. This affects how they treat customers.
- Employees shpuld be evaluated people on their capacity to understand and meet customers' needs.

- Diversity training should be an integral part of normal staff and leadership development. The training should emphasize the marketplace argument.
- To build staff commitment, approach inclusiveness as a core organizational value—not a project with a start and end point. Make inclusiveness-affirming behavior part of individual and team evaluations.

Helpful Hints

Getting Started

- **Secure CEO support to building commitment from a diverse staff.** Otherwise, your efforts will fail.
- **Dedicate specific resources.** Earmark money for funding initiatives, training programs, a library, program evaluations, and so forth. Allocate sufficient time to plan, build, and maintain every initiative.
- **Take multiple paths.** Use diversity training, cultural recognition, assessments, and change of organizational culture. Link diversity with existing initiatives to develop commitment.
- **Articulate the marketplace argument for diversity.** Make certain staff understand the necessity of making a commitment to customer service.
- **Open lines of communication with staff.** Allow them to offer suggestions and participate in efforts to change the culture. Let them express their needs—and make sure you acknowledge their concerns. Where desirable, establish affinity groups to formalize the process of collecting and sharing diverse perspectives.
- **Remember: Happy employees make happy customers.** Determine what your employees find important. Do they appreciate recognitions, rewards, or celebrations? Make sure you satisfy their needs and likes.
- **Articulate behavioral expectations.** Set inclusiveness-affirming behavior as a standard, ensuring staff know what's acceptable and unacceptable in terms of actions and language. Spell out the consequences for demeaning others.
- **Hire adaptable, flexible staff.** Share your organizational commitment with interviewees. State that your organization has made a commitment to diversity and wants to hire people who will thrive in an inclusive environment.
- **Enlist the help of specialists.** Compile a roster of consultants in diversity training and conflict management who can help you assess your organizational culture and suggest corrective action.
- **Develop a planning guide.** The guide should promote a shared sense of purpose, motivate staff, and facilitate change in the organization's culture. It should outline policies, procedures, and techniques for building an inclusive work environment.

Maintaining the Effort

- **Assess and build on existing diversity and staff development initiatives.** Sometimes strengthening what exists is better than starting a whole new effort.
- **Encourage employees to form support or affinity groups.** Allow employees to air grievances and determine ways to increase their comfort on the job.

- **Create an environment that values everyone's contributions.** Involve all employees in efforts to enhance productivity, and encourage them to voice their ideas for improving morale. When they identify problems, solicit their help in finding solutions. By all means, reward participation—and use the advice.
- **Involve employees in creating a customer-service environment.** Encourage them to identify and communicate ways to improve customer service. Make this a shared value of the organization.
- **Use employee feedback and formal assessments on organizational culture.** To gain and maintain staff commitment, it's imperative to use these tools to systematically eliminate barriers to performance.
- **Make sure your organization complies with federal, state, and corporate ordinances.** Document Americans With Disabilities (ADA) provisions, your organization's sexual harassment policy, and affirmative guidelines if applicable. Offer them to clients to review.
- **Document behavioral expectations.** Start with the employee handbook, then periodically include standards of behavior in all internal publications.
- **Educate staff about the diversity/inclusiveness effort.** Design a communications strategy that underscores the need for the diversity initiative, helps everyone understand his or her role in the effort, and emphasizes your organization's commitment and policies. Develop a slogan to use on posters and in newsletters.
- **Hold managers accountable.** Make sure managers participate in training that shows how to incorporate inclusiveness into day-to-day operations. Reward managers for their abilities to manage and understand diversity's relationship to the bottom line.
- **Don't pigeonhole employees into racial or gender classifications.** Value and respect all employees regardless of the particular group they're in. Enable employees to cross-train and develop skills in a variety of areas.
- **Build diverse teams.** Assemble cross-functional and multicultural teams to work on projects. Make the teams—not individuals—responsible for progress. Tie rewards to team gains.
- **Reward employees with opportunities to grow.** Establish mentor systems and other programs to help staff who show potential take on more responsible positions and leadership roles.
- **Let staff choose ways to celebrate differences.** Some organizations have multicultural days, where people celebrate different cultures with foods, costumes, and competitions.
- **Reward inclusive behavior.** Have policies in place so staff and management know what happens to people who consistently demonstrate inclusive behavior and those who don't. Apply the policies consistently and fairly.

- **Document staff and management's experiences.** Developing a culture that values diversity is an ongoing process. Share with everyone how well the organization is doing and show improvements.
- **Keep staff and management accountable.** Encourage them to set their own goals for individual growth and development. Help them evaluate their progress.
- **Build a diversity library.** As a starting point, refer to Appendix B.

VIGNETTES

When it comes to building commitment from a diverse staff, the following organizations prove that where there's a will, there's a way.

Making Work Relationships Succeed

AMERICAN BANKERS ASSOCIATION

The Washington, D.C.-based American Bankers Association (ABA) has had an affirmative action program since 1974. Today, however, ABA focuses on making work relationships work. The association sponsors training classes for managers, which address racial and cultural issues, and holds workshops on gender issues and on accommodating differently abled people.

ABA rewrote its job descriptions and functions to combat discrimination against differently abled people. By clarifying essential requirements, staff and managers recognized the effects of hidden bias—a wheelchair-bound person can, in fact, deliver mail, and a blind person can do word processing by using a Braille keyboard.

Tapping the Potential of All Employees

AMERICAN SPEECH LANGUAGE HEARING ASSOCIATION

Managing diversity at the American Speech-Language-Hearing Association (ASHA) in Rockville, Maryland, means fostering the development of a diverse staff, says Janet McNichol, director of human resources. The association is redefining its work culture "in terms of a shared set of values and common objectives."

To create an environment that enables all employees to do their best work, ASHA requires staff members to attend an annual program on the effects of sexual harassment and sexism in the work environment. The Americans with Disabilities Act team concentrates on improving accessibility at the association's headquarters and instructing staff. When a recruiting team interviews prospects, it includes at least one staff member of a minority group.

Creating a Participative Environment

HILTON HOTELS, EASTERN REGION

The 15 properties that make up the eastern region of Hilton Hotels have a corporate goal to create an environment where all employees participate. Managers and executive committees receive ongoing training, with new modules being designed to teach department heads how to develop and empower staff.

The effort, however, doesn't take a cookie-cutter approach, says Al Church, regional director of human resources. Each property has different needs, so a three-person committee defines the site's demographics, cultures, and so forth, before determining which strategy appears most advantageous.

Every year, the corporation holds its general managers accountable for preparing their staffs for upward mobility. Most use TQM principles, enhanced training, and education opportunities. Church says increasing the staff's level of comfort and commitment is only one benefit; providing a good work environment is also an effective recruitment tool.

Mirroring the Global Market
Levi Strauss & Company

In 1984, after several women and minorities complained to senior managers about the lack of diversity in management ranks, Levi Strauss & Company (LS&CO) held a meeting. Nineteen similar meetings followed, giving white managers and women and minorities the opportunity to discuss issues and barriers to advancement.

Those meetings resulted in the creation of Employee Forums, vehicles for a cross-section of employees to meet with a top manager monthly and discuss issues and concerns. Next came workshops for different ethnic groups and, eventually, associations for each group of employees. LS&CO then created a Diversity Council to help its leaders manage competing interests among the various affinity groups. Managers truly began paying attention to diversity issues when the company started tying a portion of every manager's bonus to the achievement of EEO goals. In this way, the company holds all senior managers accountable for meeting standards.

In 1989 LS&CO created the experiential Valuing Diversity program, which is designed to help participants explore their feelings and beliefs in regard to race, gender, ability, style, and culture. The program, offered worldwide, uses both internal and external trainers.

LS&CO values drive its key business decisions. For instance, the company chose not to do business in China because of pervasive human rights violations. In addition, LS&CO established minimum safety standards that their contractors must meet.

Each year LS&CO holds an annual succession meeting to look at moving more women and minorities into key positions. It recently launched a new marketing program directed toward the Hispanic market and uses translators or signers whenever necessary in meetings.

LS&CO's belief that it should reflect a broad representation of diversity at all levels affects the composition of its staff, the nature of its products and services, its image, and its future. The business reason for claiming diversity as a company value is simple, according to Sue Thompson, director of human resource development. "The market we serve is a diverse market, globally," she says. "The better we represent the market, the better we are able to serve it."

Solving Staff Problems

LOEWS HOTELS

Loews Corporation has conducted diversity training throughout its Loews Hotels Division since 1992. The program—which focuses on topics causing the most conflict at the particular property—has heightened management's awareness of issues affecting minority and female employees, says Ken Abrams, vice president of personnel. The training also convinced two women who had contemplated legal action against the company to resolve their issue through another means.

Loews aims its effort at helping managers perceive what they're doing to contribute to or solve staff problems. The president and senior executive officers emphasized the importance of diversity training by attending the first session. Later, the general managers and executive committee participated, followed by department managers. The program continues to cycle through management.

Valuing Diverse People and Their Talents

MARRIOTT INTERNATIONAL

Marriott International traces its official diversity efforts to 1989. Originally grounded in EEO and affirmative action goals, Marriott's initiatives no longer focus on "counting heads" but on valuing people and their talents. A diversity committee as well as leadership and advocacy support groups have helped change the organization on all levels.

Although it hasn't abandoned EEO or affirmative action legal requirements, Marriott has made awareness training a top priority and requires all general managers and the human resource directors to participate in a two-day program. Senior leaders discuss the "diversity agenda" in the field and help general managers identify relevant issues and their need for skills training. The general managers ultimately bear responsibility for obtaining results.

Marriott's chief executive officer, J. W. Marriott, Jr., favors a top-down approach, where the leaders set the example. He's committed to increasing women's and minorities' access to the company's top management levels. Over the past few years, Sandy Leandro, senior leader of diversity, has noticed some changes. "I hear people talking differently and noticing things they hadn't noticed before," she says, adding that people who make racist or sexist remarks are being challenged by their colleagues.

Starting With Staff-Driven Initiatives

NATIONAL ASSOCIATION OF HOME BUILDERS

Staff at the National Association of Home Builders (NAHB), Washington, D.C., make sensitivity issues important in day-to-day operations. From sponsoring social events that celebrate different cultures, to helping girls understand how the association serves the home-building industry, NAHB employees hope to increase awareness of gender issues. Through education they hope to develop an appreciation of cultural differences.

Because a group of employees proposed and planned an international luncheon and other activities to celebrate Black History Month in 1993, NAHB now has an employee-driven Cultural Events Committee. The committee provides advice and allocates funding to help employees of ethnic groups plan activities to share their cultures. In addition to Black History Month events, NAHB has celebrated Irish Heritage Month in March and participated in the "Take Your Daughter to Work Day" co-sponsored by the Ms. Foundation and the American Association of University Women. Along with the daughters of employees, 22 sixth-grade girls from a local school spent the day at NAHB. Dawn Harris, director of personnel, is quick to point out these efforts are still staff-driven and continue to evolve each year. Committee members have initiated outreach activities to encourage participation among various ethnic groups.

Additionally, NAHB has drafted a document that establishes guidelines for acceptable standards of interaction between staff and association members. Harris notes that many of NAHB's 300 staff members are women while most of its 180,000 members are men, so the document represents a broad-based effort to formally address gender issues and professional conduct.

Reflecting the Client Communities

NATIONAL ASSOCIATION OF SOCIAL WORKERS

The National Association of Social Workers (NASW), Washington, D.C., has focused primarily on developing an organizational culture that reflects the communities and clients it serves. Since late 1969, a comprehensive affirmative action program—and later a Minority Affairs Committee—have bolstered diversity initiatives. Both the affirmative action guidelines (which address association activities, leadership, and goals) and the committee continue to promote inclusion.

The committee, composed of six volunteers, has a broad scope of duties. It monitors the implementation of affirmative action policies, reviews public policy statements to eliminate prejudice and to address the concerns of minority groups, and collects data on immigration policies. It even works on recruitment and retention issues facing NASW's marketing office. Recently the committee has begun recommending outstanding minority people for appointments and plans special projects such as training classes, conference proceedings, workshops, and publications for minority causes.

NASW seeks proportionate representation of staff based on chapter memberships, according to Luisa Lopez, special assistant for affirmative action and affirmative action officer. NASW's leadership reflects an array of communities and cultures—African American, Mexican American, Puerto Rican and other Hispanic, Asian American/Pacific Islander, and Native American. Efforts to ensure a diverse staff in all levels of the organization have included focusing on the affirmative action policies when vacancies occur. Now NASW has large pools of applicants to choose from. Lopez says, "We work to make sure our policies don't exclude white males. They are one of the team as opposed to the predominate members."

Letting Staff Benefit From Diversity Efforts

SEATTLE-KING COUNTY CONVENTION AND VISITORS BUREAU

Although most of its diversity efforts have been aimed at building credibility and a presence in nearby ethnic communities, the staff of Washington's Seattle-King County Convention and Visitors Bureau (S-KCCVB) have benefitted as well.

Initially, Steven C. Morris, the bureau's president, insisted department heads have a good reason for not hiring a minority person when a position opened. Thanks to a three-day sensitivity training and the staff's response to it, there's no longer a need to push the hiring process to guarantee a balance of candidates. Morris believes the now ethnically diverse staff will increase commitment and ensure continuity.

The bureau has replaced its bureaucratic salary structure with rewards for individual achievement. Flex-time is available, and the bureau can customize assignments based on employee needs.

Building a Diverse Management Team

SHERATON WASHINGTON

The staff of the Sheraton Washington Hotel (SW) represent more than 55 countries. The property ensures its staff's comfort and promotes various cultures with social events, talent shows, and fashion shows. SW is involved with the National Society of Minority Hoteliers and the National Urban League, which helps its recruitment efforts. Other initiatives focus on mentoring, training for managers and support staff, and addressing issues of difference.

In addition, the hotel follows ITT Sheraton's mandate to build balanced management teams and show results, says Jesse Stewart, Jr., director of human resources. The corporation formed the Balanced Management Task Force in 1991 with the objective of attracting and retaining minority talent in the management ranks. The task force, a cross-functional, diverse group of managers, recommends strategies, says Stewart, not "minority programs that could be done away with in lean times."

Like all Sheraton managers, Stewart reports annually on SW's progress on diversity issues. ITT Sheraton uses the results in performance reviews and is developing a bonus program to reward managers' diversity efforts.

Making All Employees Comfortable in the Marketplace

WASHINGTON HILTON AND TOWERS (WH&T)

Located in the nation's capital, the Washington Hilton and Towers (WH&T) boasts a diverse staff that speaks 26 different languages. Because of the staff's diversity, management's primary task is to establish an environment of equality—not by writing a policy but by establishing a way of life.

"Long before ensuring equality became a federal rule, it was a golden rule," says William H. Edwards, Jr., general manager. Focusing on the latter concept is what enables WH&T to obtain the full support and participation of its staff, adds Edwards.

WH&T has no so-called "diversity policy." Its standard operating procedures, grounded in TQM principles, ensure that all employees feel at home and comfortable in the workplace. For starters, all employees attend a one-day orientation on the issue of equality at WH&T. Among other things, employees learn that they can lose their jobs for using slang terms that disparage a person's race or religion. The company also provides free English lessons to staff.

Managers maintain an open-door policy and meet with line employees regularly at roundtable discussions. The manager's job, says Edwards, is to listen to complaints and seize opportunities to enhance the employees' work experience. All employees who wish to move up through the ranks are matched with mentors who help them plot career paths. Additionally, employees can meet with any administrative representative, including the regional manager, human resource personnel, and department heads. The human resource office includes African Americans, Hispanics, and females; staff literally see themselves represented at the administrative level.

Hilton's regional managers monitor the progress of general managers and hold them accountable to the corporate goal of increasing minority representation at the managerial level.

CHAPTER 7

DEVELOPING INCLUSIVE BOARDS OF DIRECTORS

The same principles that apply to decision making by staff and members apply to boards of directors. Diverse boards are better able to address complicated issues involving diverse marketplaces.

Most for-profit organizations that are winning with diversity have diverse management teams and are gradually increasing the diversity of their boards of directors. Nonprofit organizations have an additional hurdle: They often recruit board members for their fund-raising abilities or personal philanthropic potential. Yet it's important that members also have the ability to relate to diverse clienteles and contributors.

If you believe the pool of accomplished women and minority persons who qualify for board positions has already been tapped out, you're not alone. Most of these people are already overcommitted. Yet in both traditional and grassroots organizations, you'll find an abundant supply of rising women and minority leaders who can be mobilized for board service.

This chapter includes a case study and two vignettes of organizations that are training nontraditional candidates to serve as board members and training traditional board members to deal with diversity. The United Way of America has implemented a program to locate, recruit, train, and place minority board members in member agencies within communities it serves; the National Center for Nonprofit Boards has made diversity a key ingredient in its ongoing training program for board members; and the Volunteer Consulting Group has developed the "Board Marketplace Program" to link nontraditional candidates with board place vacancies.

CASE STUDY

Increasing the Inclusiveness of Boards
UNITED WAY OF AMERICA

In 1987 United Way of America (UWA), headquartered in Alexandria, Virginia, formalized its efforts to increase the level of inclusiveness on its system's boards of directors. That's when it launched "Project Blueprint," which aims to accelerate involvement of African American, Asian American/Pacific Islander, Hispanic, and Native American volunteer policy makers on United Way and agency boards and committees.

Educating Communities

UWA serves as the support center by providing speakers and consultants for local chapters, sponsoring workshops, publishing a quarterly newsletter that publicizes local and national efforts and success stories, and distributing "Project Blueprint: A Plan for the Future" videotapes. The video demonstrates the need for and rewards of having diverse boards of directors. The video also sets the stage for the more challenging aspects of working toward board inclusiveness, which is the subject of UWA's two-volume set *Blueprint for Board Diversity.*

Volume 1: Volunteer Leadership Curriculum Models was designed to help "accelerate the installation of minority volunteer-leadership development programs." It provides ready-to-use training curricula for enhancing the leadership skills of minority volunteers and preparing them to serve on boards and community service positions. The first two modules cover volunteer leadership and board operations and structure. Other modules address cultural diversity and cross-cultural communications, resource development and budget concerns, and cooperative action and community problem solving. Issues of cultural diversity are more fully addressed in the second volume.

Volume 2: A Cultural Diversity Resource Manual to Improve Board Effectiveness is designed to improve communications on multicultural volunteer boards; but it can easily be adapted to suit the needs of any organization. After defining "cultural diversity," the authors tackle the tougher question of why it has to be addressed in the first place. Discussions on planning issues including using, evaluating, and interpreting survey instrument are followed with approaches to skill building. Specifically, techniques on how to conduct informational briefings, deliver training programs, and organize cultural exchanges are explained. The book concludes with recommendations for managing diversity, resources, United Way experiences in enhancing cross-cultural communication, and an inclusiveness self-assessment model.

Both texts speak volumes to staffs of local United Way agencies as well as collaborating organizations. Because UWA serves as a focal point and resource for local United Ways, communities can expect assistance in tailoring approaches that reflect their needs and circumstances. One such example follows:

The United Way of King County (UWKC): Located in Seattle, Washington, UWKC is adamant that the boards and the staffs of affiliated agencies reflect their constituency base. To help boards become diverse, UWKC launched Project LEAD (Leadership, Effectiveness, And Diversity). The project offers training for and creates partnerships between experienced volunteers from communities of color and nonprofit boards and committees. Project trainers prepare people who have a grassroots orientation to work on boards; at the same time, they debunk myths and stereotypes about board functions and increase participants' "comfort factor."

The new volunteers and agency staff attend some trainings together. Agency representatives cover topics such as the importance of cultural diversity, how to build relationships with communities of color, the responsibilities of a diverse board, cross-cultural communication skills, strategies for implementing diversity initiatives, and the financial effect of diversification. The volunteers learn about leadership and communication styles, board roles and responsibilities, committee functions, fund raising, fiduciary responsibilities, and effective nonprofit management skills.

Project LEAD participants have found that benefits run in both directions. Boards desperately need the voices of their diverse constituencies, and grassroots volunteers are heard more clearly by members of their community.

PRACTICAL APPLICATIONS

No two situations are exactly alike. The role and expectations of boards of directors vary from one situation to another. Therefore, the diversity needs of each board are distinctive and must be analyzed individually. Having said that, a monocultural board of directors that serves diverse customer or client groups will find it difficult to make good strategic decisions.

Introducing diversity on a board isn't easy. It's best addressed as part of the organization's overall diversity initiative rather than a stand-alone effort. It's also desirable to place white men and women on the boards of traditionally minority organizations. These people often bring special skills or contacts, not to mention perspectives, that can help the organization.

LESSONS LEARNED

- Community training programs are needed to identify, recruit, develop, place, and retain rising leaders. These programs make two-way connections—they work with corporations and minority and community organizations to identify board candidates, and they link those candidates to organizations requiring board members. Such programs also provide training and experience so rising leaders know what board service entails.
- Mentoring programs are essential for new, nontraditional board members. Mentoring provides opportunities for ongoing training and development and helps increase retention.
- Traditional board members need training to prepare for the changes that will come. Boards must change the way they operate as they become more diverse. For example, most board members employ a corporate, "clubby" style that they may need to modify so other board members feel comfortable.
- Diversity training programs for boards are critical. They should focus on the marketplace argument for diversity and touch on what it's like

to be different in a predominant culture. Other recommended topics include how to share leadership in a diverse setting and how to sustain the organization's commitment to diversity and inclusiveness.

Helpful Hints

Getting Started

- **Specify that developing an inclusive board is part of an ongoing commitment to inclusiveness.** Some organizations begin increasing board diversity without making an overall commitment to diversity and inclusiveness. Without sustained support throughout the organization, this approach never reaches its full potential.
- **Provide diversity training for the board.** Board members and trustees must understand the marketplace argument for diversity and how it applies to their organization, what it's like to be "different," and how they need to function differently in a more diverse setting.
- **Assess the composition of the board and the customer or client groups served.** To guide your search for board members, determine areas of desired diversity. Depending on your organization's business, trade, philanthropy, or profession, the dimensions of diversity may include gender, race or ethnicity, age, nationality, special skills, lifestyle, location, and sexual preference.
- **Use both traditional and nontraditional sources.** The traditional sources for board recommendations—business and professional contacts and "old boy" networks— typically don't yield diverse candidates, although you may get lucky. You should, therefore, identify nontraditional sources in your community, such as organizations serving racial or ethnic minorities and women as well as corporations that can recommend diverse candidates.
- **Assign mentors for diverse board members.** Select the mentors wisely and provide training on what is expected of them.

Maintaining the Effort

- **Change the culture to be comfortable for a diverse membership.** Refer to Chapters 2 through 6 for tips you can apply to your board's culture and meetings.
- **Develop a library of helpful readings.** Appendix B contains recommended references.

Vignettes

Tailoring Diversity Programs to Needs

NATIONAL CENTER FOR NONPROFIT BOARDS (NCNB)

The National Center for Nonprofit Boards (NCNB), Washington, D.C., develops publications, information resources, and training and education programs to help boards increase their effectiveness. Increasingly, an organization's credibility and effectiveness is tied to its commitment—at both the board and staff levels—to reflect the community or constituency it serves.

As part of its Building Board Diversity project, funded by the Ford Foundation, NCNB examined the status of diversity among boards and explored the sector's need for information and technical assistance. The results? The techniques that strengthen overall board effectiveness—good recruitment strategies, comprehensive orientation programs for new members, continuing education for current members, and well-structured board and committee work—are critical factors in attracting and retaining the people who contribute to a board's diversity.

In addition to the published results of this research, the center offers workshops and board-development programs on this issue.

Developing a Marketplace for Board Members

VOLUNTEER CONSULTING GROUP

The Volunteer Consulting Group (VCG), headquartered in New York City, has long conducted trainings and offered matchmaking services for nonprofit boards. In recent years, it has become involved in a major initiative funded by the W. K. Kellogg Foundation to identify, recruit, train, place, and retain nontraditional board members. VCG also addresses how to achieve diversity within a board without losing the ability of all the board members to work together.

As a result of the initiative, VCG has developed a model for building bridges into and out of the board marketplace—the junction between organizations needing board members and the pool of people available to serve. VCG has also developed mentoring programs and other initiatives to prepare new board members for their assignments and to prepare the new board to accept the new members.

In these changing times, VCG doesn't recommend that boards continue to conduct business as usual. Instead, the group advises, boards must do the following:
- Change their membership.
- Change the manner in which they function.
- Share leadership among different board members.

CHAPTER 8

ENSURING THE INCLUSIVENESS OF THE WORKFORCE OF THE FUTURE

Many types of organizations are ensuring that capable people who reflect the diversity of the population find their way into the related industry or profession's employment pipeline. These initiatives typically involve partnerships.

As an example, the following case study summarizes efforts of two engineering societies and two institutions to increase the numbers of women and minorities who enter and succeed in the field. This complex endeavor illustrates how schools, employers, community organizations, and associations can work together to address diversity issues.

CASE STUDY

Preparing Engineers for the Future

The engineering profession's effort to increase career opportunities for women and minorities has dovetailed with broad national efforts to increase opportunities in math- and science-related careers for underrepresented groups. Virtually all of the national professional and governmental organizations dealing with science and mathematics, community-based organizations, colleges and universities, and elementary and secondary schools have gotten involved.

Their joint efforts have yielded three insights:

1. Barriers to success for underrepresented minorities and women extend all the way from preschool to the workforce. People at different levels and in different groups encounter different barriers, including issues of preparation, expectations, esteem building, mentoring, socialization, and cultural change.
2. Solutions require partnerships among organizations that span the full range and scope of the issues.
3. Organizations need examples of success stories to illustrate the roles they can play, in conjunction with other organizations, to make the math- and science-related workforce of the future inclusive.

The experiences of the following organizations mirror these insights.

Targeting Women and Youth

NATIONAL SOCIETY OF PROFESSIONAL ENGINEERS

The National Society of Professional Engineers (NSPE) cosponsors two national engineering programs to strengthen math and science achievement among inner-city youth and to excite all children about engineering as a career. NSPE's executive director, Donald G. Weinert, acknowledges the need to eliminate the barriers that women and minorities face in the academic and professional culture of engineers. He says that efforts to address disparities should be made on multiple fronts—including the early years of childhood.

NSPE recently published "The Glass Ceiling and Women in Engineering," which details findings from focus groups and a survey of chief executive officers and human resource managers in private practice and in construction firms. The results show that the respondents employ a small number of women engineers and that only 25 percent of female engineers in private practice hold management positions. CEO respondents said the most compelling reason to help women engineers advance into top management positions is the need to develop the highest quality workforce.

NSPE plans to produce a video and complementary text module. Its goal: to help raise individual and corporate awareness of the gender bias that erects an artificial barrier to the professional advancement of women engineers. Several foundations have contributed financial support to this project.

NSPE doesn't advocate a particular approach to encouraging young people to examine engineering as a possible career. "No single model works in every community, so we have to tailor approaches to local conditions," says Weinert. The society has "adopted" an elementary school near its headquarters in Alexandria, Virginia, providing equipment and engineers who serve as mentors. NSPE also plans to increase exposure of minority students to community-based competitions of national engineering programs.

NSPE serves as the secretariat of Engineers Week, an annual campaign to help improve the public's understanding of and appreciation for the engineering profession. Participants in the related "Discover 'E'" programs use model bridge-building contests and other hands-on activities to show students and teachers the practical applications of math and science. During the week, students visit technology centers and engineering project sites and meet role models. In turn, engineers go into classrooms to get students interested in some facet of science and engineering, such as using computer programs and models to design futuristic cities.

NSPE also cosponsors MATHCOUNTS, a national program to increase American students' mathematics achievement. So far, says Weinert, females represent about 40 percent of local participants, although few minorities participate. To change that, the MATHCOUNTS board is actively recruiting more females and minorities to serve as role models and volunteers. MATHCOUNTS also sponsors teacher workshops geared toward increasing the involvement of girls and minorities.

Partnering With the Pros

NATIONAL ACTION COUNCIL FOR MINORITIES IN ENGINEERING, INC.

The National Action Council for Minorities in Engineering, Inc. (NACME) is a nonprofit corporation, headquartered in New York, NY. NACME develops and operates programs to increase the number of African-American, Hispanic, and Native-American engineers. In addition to providing scholarships, publishing materials, and conducting workshops, the organization sponsors public policy research and recommends novel ways to teach math and science in schools. To fund these programs, NACME fosters partnerships that lead to innovative problem solving and provide access to state-of-the-art equipment.

The programs target students (at the primary, secondary, and college levels), teachers, and parents. For example, NACME's McAllen/Mission Mathematics and Science Project provides professional and curriculum development for fourth-, fifth-, and sixth-grade teachers in a Mexican-American community. With "Say YES Through Family Math and Family Science," NACME and the National Urban Coalition forge partnerships among parents, teachers, and schools. The program provides teacher training and sponsors after-school activities for parents and children. NACME's latest joint venture, TechForce Partnership for Scientific Learning, emphasizes the all-children-can-learn philosophy in two New York City elementary schools. The program includes instructional and leadership training for teachers.

To introduce minority youngsters to careers in engineering, NACME worked with Marvel Comics to publish *Chaos at the Construction Site* and *Riot at RobotWorld*. The comic books feature action-packed story lines and young minority engineers as characters who help Spider Man save the day. Also for 10- to 13-year-olds, NACME produced "The Challenge." In this video, the young hero is trapped inside a video game—and must learn about careers in engineering in order to escape. The video also features six minority engineers describing their work, its importance, and obstacles they've encountered.

Two NACME programs place and support outstanding and culturally diverse engineering students. As an added benefit, these programs help enrich the university environment. This partnership recruits students and, for eight months, helps them refine leadership skills, expand academic proficiency, explore concepts in engineering, and develop group cohesiveness. According to NACME, students who enter engineering schools together will remain strongly committed to obtaining an engineering education. They're also armed with a support network and full scholarships. The first group of 10 multicultural inner-city students participating in the Engineering Posse Program begin studying at Rice University in 1994.

In cooperation with 15 corporations, NACME sponsors more than 120 corporate scholars. These high-achieving engineering students—who are

African American, Hispanic, and Native American—receive financial aid linked to their grade-point average. The Corporate Scholars Program also provides academic enrichment, corporate experience, mentors, career guidance, and leadership training. In turn, the corporations can steer scholars toward the engineering areas with the greatest personnel needs.

NACME has also turned its attention to the engineering schools. The council recently introduced diversity seminars to help increase the sensitivity of faculty members and first-year minority students. During the sessions, participants role play while exploring issues of bias and ethnic stereotyping that affect the faculty-student relationship. The seminars also help faculty build skills in counseling.

Together with an impressive list of donors, NACME has implemented numerous other strategies related to research scholarships, program development, communications, and public affairs. All are intended to increase the number of diverse engineers, fund minority engineering students, improve retention, and expand the educational pipeline to yield a steady stream of world-class engineers.

Retaining Minority Students

GEORGIA INSTITUTE OF TECHNOLOGY

Georgia Institute of Technology has about 9,000 undergraduates and 3,000 graduate students. Except for the University of Puerto Rico in Mayaguez, Georgia Tech enrolls and awards bachelor's degrees to more underrepresented minorities than any other American university.

Still, the high attrition rate among minority students—despite special mentoring and support programs—concerned the school's Office of Minority Educational Development (OMED). The staff applied principles of continuous quality improvement (CQI) to analyze the problem and craft a solution.

Their analysis showed three predominant reasons for poor academic performance:
1. The students were poorly prepared for the Georgia Tech system.
2. The students and others had low expectations for their success.
3. The students didn't study in groups.

OMED responded with a three-point plan. First, the office identified important transitions that students needed to successfully navigate through high school and other colleges: chemistry to physics, physics to statics/dynamics and thermodynamics, introductory science to major engineering courses, and undergraduate to graduate.

Second, they identified programs that help students navigate these transitions, including support groups, student coaching, information kits, and grade monitoring. Third, they involved parents through grade-release forms, phone calls, visits, letters, and newsletters. In the spirit of CQI,

OMED specified that it would judge its performance by an increase in the retention rate of minority students.

The results? The performance of minority students has improved markedly. Retention has improved. In fact, freshman-year retention for minority students is higher than similar measures for majority students. The program has been so successful that Georgia Tech may apply it to improve freshman-year transitions for all students.

Georgia Tech has established the production of minority and women graduates as a strategic priority. It remains publicly committed to becoming the top producer of minority PhDs in technical disciplines. Georgia Tech's initiatives have also attracted media attention—an article in a *U.S. News and World Report* issue on the nation's best colleges.

Creating Effective Learning Environments

CALIFORNIA STATE UNIVERSITY-LOS ANGELES

The approximately 20,000 students who attend California State University at Los Angeles (CSU-LA) reflect the diversity of the area's population. Significant numbers of African American, Hispanic, Asian American, and international students attend the university; many of the best major in engineering.

CSU-LA joins other campuses in the California State and University of California systems in participating in the Minority Education Program (MEP). Minority students in the MEP have higher retention rates than other minority students; as a group, their retention rates are higher than those for majority students.

MEP's goal is to create a model learning environment. The first component involves building a collaborative learning environment where students work together and use structured study groups. An orientation course for minority engineering freshmen focuses on community building, academic survival skills, personal development, professional development, and orientation to the university and its engineering school. Further aids include structured study groups, a student study center, and student support services.

PRACTICAL APPLICATIONS

Partnering is essential for ensuring that your industry or profession will have access to a sufficient number of qualified employees who reflect the workforce of the future. The goal should be to identify and then strengthen the weak links—where potential workers get lost in the system or culture.

LESSONS LEARNED

- The more extensive the educational requirements of the profession, the earlier interventions must occur. Elementary school initiatives, for example, both develop interest in the profession and ensure that students will be qualified.
- National efforts to develop a professional pipeline are useful. They can provide an umbrella organization, networks, models for success, and sometimes funding. The real action, however, occurs locally.
- More partnerships among diverse community organizations are developing to deal with the skills of elementary and high school students. Organizations should link up with these existing partnerships.
- Links with local colleges and universities—especially those with historically black and Hispanic enrollments—are useful mechanisms to enhance recruitment.
- Organizations must show employees that they're serious about removing barriers to successful performance and ensuring growth and promotional opportunities. Initiatives to support the diversity of the "pipeline" demonstrate that commitment.

HELPFUL HINTS

Getting Started

- **Obtain commitment from leaders in the profession, trade, philanthropy, or business.** Without that commitment, these initiatives are merely window dressing. It will be necessary to identify the size of the gap and the factors that may prevent your industry or profession from tapping the full potential of the future workforce.
- **Assess the current diversity of your pipeline.** Compare the results to appropriate benchmarks. How well does your organization, profession, or trade reflect the diversity of the workforce at large? Depending on the skills and education requirements, you may need to trace the pipeline from elementary school through high school, college, and even graduate school.
- **Identify the reasons for your workforce disparity.** These may include a lack of awareness of the opportunities in your profession, trade, or philanthropy; lack of adequate numbers of skilled applicants; failure to tap existing labor pools; and barriers within your workforce. Or perhaps your profession's reputation makes it unattractive to diverse employees.
- **Learn from the efforts of other professions.** Whatever your trade, profession, philanthropy, or business, a peer organization has probably undertaken initiatives to develop the employment pipeline.

- **Launch an awareness program or expand existing awareness efforts.** Your existing awareness program and recruitment materials may suffer from communication weaknesses. Create materials that advance your image as an industry or profession that respects and values diversity (see Chapter 4).
- **Develop the pipeline of skilled applicants.** How deep into the pipeline do you need to extend your recruitment and improvement efforts? The answer will vary, depending on the adequacy of the existing pool of diverse, skilled applicants. Some professions may only need to enhance their recruiting and image-building efforts. Others, such as engineering and the health sciences, may need to actively support skills development and mentoring programs as far down as elementary school.
- **Develop training and professional development programs for current employees.** Remember: You'll find your best source of skilled workers and leaders among your current staff.
- **Remove barriers to the recruitment and advancement of diverse workers.** To truly improve the pipeline for diverse workers, the industry or profession must systematically remove the barriers to advancement that fall most heavily on diverse workers. (NSPE's work on the glass ceiling for women in engineering is a case in point.)

Maintaining the Effort

- **Commission ongoing research to determine emerging challenges.** Once you've begun an effort, continue it. The engineering and medical professions continually work on identifying challenges that diverse workers face.
- **Form alliances with other professional associations.** Also engage in local partnerships to improve educational preparation and professional awareness of diverse populations. In most cases, producing a skilled, diverse workforce proves a bigger challenge than any single organization can undertake. Partnerships and alliances—especially those that involve local activities—make it possible for people to participate easily, in their own communities.
- **Involve as many members as possible.** When your members work with young people, they'll develop a personal stake in increasing the diversity of tomorrow's workforce. This personal involvement will create a legion of committed professionals who support your efforts to create a skilled, diverse workforce within the trade or profession.
- **Emphasize not just skills, but the shared values and socialization of your industry or profession.** These shared values will bind together the increasing diverse participants in tomorrow's workforce.

The following organizations have committed resources to building a workforce pipeline for their respective industries.

Addressing a Disparity in Employment

AMERICAN HOSPITAL ASSOCIATION

With a membership comprising 5,800 organizations and 50,000 individuals and an $85 million annual budget, the Chicago-based American Hospital Association (AHA) is well-positioned to keep tabs on its trade. After amending the bylaws in 1993 to ensure racial, ethnic, and gender equity in its governance structure, AHA became committed to the concept of inclusiveness in the field of hospital management as well. In the same year, AHA cosponsored a nationwide survey with the American College of Health Care Executives and the National Association of Health Services Executives.

Results showed that minorities represent less than 1 percent of hospital management. To address this disparity, the three organizations founded the Institute for Diversity and Health Management (IDHM). The institute is designed to usher black and Hispanic students into appropriate graduate and undergraduate programs. One IDHM program, Operation REACH (Real Equity Allows Career Heights), provides grants, tuition assistance, tutoring, and scholarships to help participants understand and pursue careers in healthcare administration. It also pays work-study students to gain experience in different hospital jobs.

IDHM supports minorities already in the workforce, too. It has developed a job bank/personnel database to help graduates find middle- and senior-level jobs. The institute also conducts seminars on career and behavior assessments and on how to prepare for work in a hospital environment.

AHA leaders believe that a diverse administrative workforce is a critical component in dealing with the restructuring of healthcare in America. Communities must see their numbers and kind reflected in the hospitals serving them. Furthermore, it makes good business sense to develop programs that attract and prepare community representatives to participate in preventive and health promotion activities.

Building an Inclusive Profession

AMERICAN PHYSICAL THERAPY ASSOCIATION

Leaders of the American Physical Therapy Association (APTA) were sensitive to issues of diversity and inclusion before 1988. But that year marked the insertion of diversity programming into the goals and objectives of the association's strategic plan and environmental statement. Today the CEO, board of directors, Advisory Panel on Minority Affairs, and department of minority/international affairs of the Alexandria, Virginia-based association are visibly working to build a more inclusive profession and to raise awareness among APTA's 140 employees, 63,000 members, 52 chapters, 19 special interest sections, and two assemblies.

In addition to giving speeches and recruiting minority members for committees, the CEO works with minority caucuses in the nation's capital. The advisory panel meets regularly and emphasizes the importance of having minorities on leadership positions. Johnette L. Meadows, director of the department of minority/international affairs, says APTA's initiatives target Asian Americans/Pacific Islanders, African Americans, Hispanic/Latinos, and Native Americans/Alaskan Natives.

Different healthcare issues and approaches arise in different cultures. "If we're not aware of differences, we can't give the best treatment," says Meadows. She adds that addressing diversity is more a professional than a social issue. So while APTA focuses on leadership internally, it focuses on education externally. Representatives of APTA speak to students about the profession and educate community groups about entry requirements. Other activities include developing programs to cultivate cultural sensitivity among students, interns, and clinicians; conducting workshops to recruit minority students and faculty; raising money for scholarships for minority students; and educating counselors and college admissions officers about the field.

Attracting Minority Student Employees
NATIONAL ASSOCIATION OF COLLEGE STORES

Through its research and education foundation, the National Association of College Stores (NACS), Oberlin, Ohio, established a fund to promote diversity. One initiative involves inviting minority student employees to attend NACS annual meetings, where they can learn more about the industry and become comfortable in it. In 1993, one seminar at the NACS annual meeting featured potential industry role models and a discussion of career opportunities. The students also spent a day at the trade show, accompanied by a guide who explained the different segments of the industry and how they fit together.

NACS has set a goal to increase diversity on its professional staff but hasn't been successful in attracting qualified candidates. After questioning minority opinion leaders, NACS decided to test messages on a local black radio station and in a black/Hispanic newspaper.

Recruiting Via a Minority Weekend Program
WASHINGTON HILTON AND TOWERS (WH&T)

Through the Minority Weekend Program, students attending the school of hotel management at a university in the Washington, D.C., area, can spend two days with minority managers, sales representatives, and other employees of the Washington Hilton and Towers (WH&T). The program enables students to get a "real world view" and ask questions about the profession. In turn, the hotel staff benefit by getting feedback from the students, which helps them create an environment that attracts minority graduates.

WH&T also participates in job fairs and career planning days at area high schools. These activities enable the property to develop ties to the community as well as provide role models for the people it may one day employ or serve as guests.

CHAPTER 9

BUILDING A COMMUNITY OF COMMUNITIES

N o organization is an island. Leading-edge associations and corporations understand that they must demonstrate their diversity commitment to the communities in which they're located. That translates into sponsoring philanthropic activities and community initiatives—and including employees or members as participants in the programs.

In earlier chapters, the case studies describe several efforts to convey organizational commitment through local community development. The case studies in this chapter focus on two national organizations whose mission involves building community within communities across the nation. The first describes the efforts of the Girl Scouts of the U.S.A. to make inclusiveness a pervasive organizational value; the second tells how the United Way of America has established diversity and inclusiveness as core values for affiliates to embrace.

CASE STUDY

GIRL SCOUTS OF THE U.S.A.

Institutionalizing Pluralism

At the New York City headquarters of Girls Scouts of the U.S.A. (GSUSA), staff no longer speak in terms of "diversity" when describing their mission to prepare girls for the future and to help them grow to become responsible women. According to Leslie Saunders, director of the pluralism strategy unit, the organization's goal of institutionalized pluralism is a process that will result in everyone—including whites—feeling valued and recognizing the benefits of inclusion.

GSUSA began developing recruitment strategies for girls of underrepresented groups long ago, in 1917. Today, it focuses on developing and advancing strategies to institutionalize the process of pluralism throughout all levels of Girl Scouting. This means promoting inclusion in membership and staff recruitment as well as developing relationships within underrepresented communities.

Ensuring an Inclusive Membership and Staff

To recruit underrepresented groups, GSUSA developed guidelines, conducted conferences and special programs, and published targeted brochures. But the results of several surveys indicated more was needed. Rather than just publicizing its intentions, the organization had to design and implement specific strategies for reaching girls who are physically challenged, aren't white, and aren't middle class.

To prevent these efforts from being viewed as temporary or ancillary programs, GSUSA integrated them into standard operating procedures. Now, says Saunders, the work has to "be done from the top down, the bottom up, and sideways." In fact, GSUSA attributes much of its success in becoming an inclusive organization to internal structures and policies. These ensure that everyone in the organization is committed to eliminating all forms and appearances of exclusion.

The CEO and the volunteer president share responsibility for the policy and operational efforts of GSUSA, which oversees 331 local councils. Saunders heads a strategy development team composed of staff from different operational functions and of national board members. The team monitors, reviews, and revises strategies. Line and staff managers are held accountable for ensuring an atmosphere of inclusion. And volunteer presidents and CEOs of local councils also get involved in spreading the word about inclusion, even if their area has a homogeneous population. Everyone in Girl Scouting has to know about pluralism and its benefits.

Initially, the group depended almost exclusively on external consultants, trainers, and materials (including diversity training videos and antibias curricula). In 1990 GSUSA began to create its own materials and, two years later, staged a think tank on pluralism. Volunteer leaders gathered with outside experts to develop recommendations on how to institutionalize pluralism. The result: a three-year strategy.

The plan includes a communications component. Specifically, it calls for designing and printing marketing resources in different languages, for different races, and for different religious groups. GSUSA also will publish a manual on *Successful Self-Management in a Diverse Workplace*.

GSUSA values an inclusive staff as much as an inclusive membership. Saunders lists an array of programs designed to promote inclusiveness, including career management programs and a networking conference for executive staff and councils that represent African American, Native American, Asian American, and Hispanic girls. A mentoring program to accelerate the careers of nonwhites is in place, as are courses to enhance the skills of white staff who don't have experience dealing with diverse populations.

With outside funding, GSUSA actively recruits nonwhite women to serve as council executive directors or other professional staff. GSUSA also offers local councils a comprehensive course on institutionalizing pluralism; it takes two to three years to complete. Participants learn about language (what you can and cannot say), how to do their jobs better, strategies for fund raising and recruitment, and how to reeducate people already affiliated with Girl Scouting.

Reaching Out to All Communities

The organization reflects its commitment to inclusion "in the vendors with whom we do business, on our national and local boards of directors, and by the organizations with whom we collaborate," says Saunders. She believes GSUSA's strongest effort comes through its diversity analysis and planning process, which includes reviewing policies and guidelines regarding how the organization presents itself to the public. Analyses focus on how people of all population groups contribute at different levels of the organization.

Each local council conducts a self-evaluation every six years. The process includes analyzing publications and pictures to find out how well girls of diverse backgrounds are represented on the board of directors and executive positions.

Saunders characterizes the changes in Girl Scouting during the last 20 years as phenomenal, adding that they've affected all aspects of how the organization conducts business. The latest statistics show membership among underrepresented girls and adults has increased. Finally, GSUSA has sponsored research with the Wellesley Center for Research of Women on racial and ethnic diversity in Scouting; with the American Association of University Women it plans to cosponsor a study of gender equity issues. These partnerships and survey results confirm GSUSA's direction and validate for corporate sponsors that Girl Scouting is a worthwhile community investment.

Having registered success in recruiting black and Native American girls, as well as girls who have physical challenges, GSUSA is addressing special needs groups in southern California, southern Texas, and Appalachia. With its latest pilot project, "Cityforce 2000," GSUSA hopes to develop a model for establishing a committed and trusted presence in urban areas.

Saunders believes it costs less to cultivate an environment of inclusion than to exclude people. "When everyone is working on the same thing, they all can feel valued and included. When the system excludes or promotes tokenism, you have divided resources," she says. Simply put: Separate and unequal costs much more.

CASE STUDY

UNITED WAY OF AMERICA

Building the Problem-Solving Capacity of Communities

Diversity represents neither a new effort nor a one-time initiative for United Way of America (UWA), Alexandria, Virginia, and its local members. Administrators constantly shape, review, and implement policies that affect all departments, employees, and agencies associated with UWA. In 1993 UWA's Diversity Task Force released a report that included strategies for furthering national and local efforts to value and manage diversity. The strategies relate to the areas of meetings, communications, staff and board development, and future workforce and community cultivation.

Meeting Attendees All the Way

A diverse committee develops plans and marketing strategies for each national conference, which ensures inclusion of broad perspectives and ideas. The planners encourage a diverse mix of meeting participants by inviting volunteers and executive directors from around the world.

UWA also invites staff and volunteers from various levels to attend its leadership conferences. In 1994 planners devoted one general session to discussing the business-related realities of diversity issues; copies of the videotape were made available to all United Ways. The conference agenda allocated time for cultural groups to meet separately, and CEOs met as a group to discuss efforts aimed at recruiting minority professionals. Also, minority executive staff and volunteers sponsored a reception designed to update all attendees on efforts to support minority professionals.

Creating Communications

The national headquarters disseminates information in several languages and in large type to accommodate older readers. UWA is concerned that all communications adequately portray and speak to diverse audiences. For example, a quarterly newsletter showcases diversity activities at the national and local levels and features faces of many colors.

UWA recently produced "Project Blueprint: A Plan for the Future" and circulated it to local United Ways. The video is designed to pique interest in and emphasize the importance of inclusiveness as it relates to board development. Related resources include a two-volume set entitled *Blueprint for Board Diversity*. One volume is a cultural diversity resource guide for developing effective boards, and the other includes training curriculum models for volunteer leaders. The national office is collaborating with members in Miami and Los Angeles to produce a fund-raising video in Spanish.

Although it relies on *The Associated Press Stylebook* to guide its communications, UWA uses an in-house supplement to address inclusiveness issues. Developed by UWA's editorial staff, with advice from UWA's general counsel and human resource staff, the supplement covers when to use terms such as black or African American, chair (instead of chairman or chairwoman), Hispanic or Latino, and Native American. It also discusses the use of preferred terms, such as "people with disabilities" instead of "the disabled."

It's not always possible to use terms that everyone approves of, concedes John Libby, senior associate, editorial review. But UWA writers follow guidelines that say manuscripts should be clear, understandable, not biased, and useful to the greatest number of people. The editor makes sure the document matches the appropriate educational level of the reader and double checks any art accompanying the text: Is it inclusive?

For years, local United Ways have tailored their publications and campaign information to suit particular clients, says Mary Williams Stover, director for diversity. The Los Angeles United Way, for example, produces publications in two or three languages. Staff of the United Way in Seattle have learned to choose their words carefully when developing recruitment materials and applications. They found that the term "leader" wasn't appropriate in some Asian communities and that many people of color don't characterize their service to churches or parent-teacher associations as "volunteer experience."

Building Staff Commitment

UWA takes a multi-level approach to building an inclusive staff:

- **Support the development of individuals.** Through a management training series and courses, consultants and in-house trainers keep staff and volunteers up-to-date on diversity issues.

In addition to providing career counseling for all staff, UWA has a Minority Leadership Development Program for nonwhite professional staff with at least three years' experience. Those wishing to advance professionally can undertake a three-year program that involves intensive training in leadership issues and presentation skills. Participants are assigned mentors, and their supervisors must agree to support their professional growth by allowing them time to participate and by giving them relevant assignments. Some use the program to diversify professionally; for example, an employee working in the finance area may want to gain fund-raising experience without losing ground in his or her current position.

- **Support the development of the organization.** Since 1983 UWA has sponsored an annual Minority Roundtable, which brings together more than 100 professionals. For $2^{1}/_{2}$ days, they identify and address issues affecting minorities in the United Way system. This enables UWA leaders to learn about the perceptions and experiences of minorities. An added bonus: participants have the opportunity to network with senior executives and to discuss career development issues. Other development programs are in place to increase the diversity of boards and committees.

- **Change the system.** In addition to the strategies proposed by the Diversity Task Force, UWA relies on its aware and active workforce to change the environment.

Increasing Inclusiveness Among Members

Bill Mills, vice president of external human resources diversity, describes UWA as a focal point, role model, trainer, and clearinghouse for local United Ways. UWA produces books, newsletters, and videos for nationwide use and provides local trainings on the benefits of becoming a diverse organization. All UWA conferences have sessions related to volunteer and staff diversity.

Local United Ways can use national resources to draft a strategic plan and assess their progress in becoming an inclusive organization. A cultural audit, for example, is recommended as the first step in developing policies and guidelines related to board governance, staff inclusiveness, and vendor relationships.

Building Inclusiveness Within the Community

UWA's emphasis on inclusiveness reminds its local members to involve their communities—particularly minority members—in all aspects of their operations. Local United Ways have responded with a variety of programs, not under the mantle of "diversity initiatives" but rather "good business practices." Their inclusiveness strategies have included building relationships with minority vendors and acknowledging ethnic markets.

UWA promotes these commitments so others can learn by example. In Minneapolis and Louisville, for example, any agency funded by the United Way must document its policies for dealing with minority vendors. The United Way of Indianapolis goes one step further, tracking its expenditures with minority vendors. UWA also participates in the Black Expo—a community event that develops visibility for black vendors and entrepreneurs—and acknowledges the service of outstanding minority volunteers through a formal recognitions program.

As another means of broadening participation within communities, UWA has explored the development of ethnic and cultural markets. National staff developed a resource manual that explores how local United Ways can effectively segment their markets and enhance fund-raising opportunities.

Focusing on the Bottom Line

Stover reports that UWA's diversity programs continue to be successful. She's seen positive changes in the way managers and staff relate to one another, how allocations are made, and how communities perceive local United Ways. Not only has the number of minority staff increased but also the number of volunteers has grown.

Encouraged by such tangible progress, UWA's CEO continues to champion the benefits and value of diversity. At the national level the organization allocated more than $100,000 to diversity programs in 1993. The nature of UWA's products and services, its image, and its future all are affected by the goal to become a more inclusive organization, says Stover: "We depend on representing the communities we serve."

Practical Applications

Every organization can benefit from building greater community among its different internal communities.

Lessons Learned

- Organizations need to demonstrate their commitment to the communities in which they function. This is an important ingredient in being seen as a "good corporate citizen" and a contributor to community well-being.
- Building bridges to the community provides the opportunity to acquaint employees with many different types of people and experiences. Used properly, it can be a broadening and enriching experience that will enhance the capacity of employees to serve diverse customers.

Helpful Hints

Getting Started

- **Develop commitment from leadership to internal and external community development.** This can be tied to commitment for other parts of your diversity and inclusiveness-building programs.
- **Use community development activities to make employees comfortable with diversity.** Everyone has a great deal to learn about different experiences—and community involvement provides a useful mechanism for doing so.

Maintaining the Effort

- **Continually assess existing community service and development programs.** Determine levels of participation, appropriateness of activities, and outcomes. Set high standards for your investment in community development, and continually review your efforts to enhance outcomes.
- **Recognize the importance of community-building activities.** Invest greater resources and encourage more staff to participate in these efforts. Community building not only contributes immediately to organizational image but also, over the long run, increases staff's ability to deal effectively with diverse people.

VIGNETTES

The efforts of the following groups underscore this truth: Every organization is part of a larger organization or setting.

Using Employee Associations for Affinity Groups

KAISER PERMANENTE HEALTH CARE PROGRAM

The diversity effort at Kaiser Permanente started with the creation of a National Diversity Council, whose first task was to determine if a business imperative existed to address diversity. The national council, which eventually spawned five regional groups, developed courses in diversity management, prepared a "business imperative" document, and created a film showing how certain administrative circumstances can block access to delivery systems.

The CEO speaks frequently of Kaiser's efforts to link culturally diverse employees with the delivery of high-quality care. By voicing this commitment, the CEO ensures the diversity effort isn't viewed as a stand-alone program. Instead, it's "part of the foundation and fabric of our organization," says Alva Wheatley, vice president and manager of the cultural diversity project.

As an example of Kaiser's effort to recruit, train, and maintain employees that reflect its membership, Wheatley points to the employee associations that exist for African Americans, Asian Americans, Latinos, bisexuals, gays, and lesbians. Also, regional managers have begun to build relationships with ethnic graduate students in healthcare and business administration programs; Kaiser often offers them jobs upon graduation.

Using Minority and Women Contractors

NATIONAL ASSOCIATION OF BROADCASTERS

Although it has no special diversity initiative in place, the Washington, D.C.-based National Association of Broadcasters (NAB) has made a commitment to using minority vendors, placing minorities in the industry, and increasing the numbers of black and female owners of radio and television stations.

Its purchasing department, for example, has successfully located minority contractors who fulfill price and quality requirements. NAB's Employment Clearinghouse solicits resumes from people of color and women broadcasters and then helps place them in all levels of the industry. And, through its relationship with civil rights organizations, NAB sponsors an organization whose sole purpose is to help minorities acquire radio stations.

Serving Client Communities

NATIONAL ASSOCIATION OF SOCIAL WORKERS

At the National Association of Social Workers (NASW), Washington, D.C., the affirmative action mandate applies to all association functions.

In addition to making events comfortable for everyone, NASW aims to achieve proportionate representation on boards of directors, community committees, and education boards. NASW's affirmative action policy extends to all business relationships, meaning that vendors must comply with EEO principles.

NASW insists that its local chapters comply and publicizes efforts of those that address minority affairs. If a chapter fails to address affirmative action goals, NASW can withhold its membership dues rebate.

With diverse representation, NASW chapters can work more effectively in the community, says Luisa Lopez, special assistant for affirmative action and affirmative action officer. "A good number of our clients are minorities. It's our commitment that clients have rights of self-determination and begin to effect the change they need." She adds, "It makes us more effective in the minority community to be able to train people to do things for themselves."

Being a more diverse organization helps overcome the ever-present barriers to communication. Additionally, many issues of trust can be overcome when facilitators resemble the racial or cultural group they're working with. Lopez, however, is quick to add that facilitators and clients aren't necessarily of the same group.

Representing, Serving, and Advancing the Community

PHILADELPHIA CONVENTION AND VISITORS BUREAU

In the mid-1980s, the president of the Philadelphia Convention and Visitors Bureau (PCVB) met with a state representative and a local businessman to discuss the lack of minority representation in the programs, management, and sales departments of the city's hospitality industry. The meeting prompted PCVB to create its Minority Advisory Committee (MAC) and implement several initiatives that bound the bureau to the community.

The committee initially focused on bringing more minority conventions into Philadelphia; marketing efforts included producing a film that highlighted the city's African-American history. It also created a brochure that described Philadelphia's various cultural groups, again highlighting the African-American experience. PCVB's sales staff, in partnership with the MAC board, actively courted black organizations. Once more minority organizations began bringing conventions to the city, MAC published a directory of local minority vendors. At the same time, the committee has conducted seminars aimed at assisting minority- and women-owned businesses. MAC doesn't miss an opportunity to spread the news that valuing diversity translates into "green power" and success for city businesses.

In 1991 the U.S. Department of Commerce designated Philadelphia as the top city for minority tourism. By 1994 Philadelphia had topped the $200 million mark in minority meetings and conventions booked in the city. In the process, PCVB has achieved more visibility and prominence as a leader in the community.

MAC has also given a stronger voice to minorities in the hospitality industry, says Thomas O. Muldoon, PCVB's president. For instance, the committee supports programs aimed at educating minority youngsters about career possibilities; magnet schools created by the Philadelphia School district and the Philadelphia Archdiocese enable high school students to learn about jobs in the hospitality industry. And, through the Hospitality Training Institute of the Opportunities Industrialization Center, underemployed persons can prepare for positions in the industry.

MAC, which has changed its name to the Multicultural Affairs Congress, is working with the Pennsylvania Historical and Museum Commission and the National Trust for Historic Preservation to develop new minority tourism sites and to improve services at existing sites. Aiming to duplicate the advances that African Americans have made within the industry, MAC plans to introduce programs for Americans of Puerto Rican/Latino and Asian descent.

Showcasing Diversity in the Community
SEATTLE-KING COUNTY CONVENTION AND VISITORS BUREAU

For the Seattle-King County Convention and Visitors Bureau (S-KCCVB), the wake-up call came from minority-elected officials who voted on budget allocations. They pressured the bureau to establish a broader base in several ethnic communities and to create awareness among citizens about its importance. S-KCCVB responded by instituting changes that have made it a more diverse organization.

To increase minority representation on the board, the bureau recruited an African-American male to serve on the executive committee and a Japanese-American woman to chair the board. A new division—the Minority Business Development Program—has done the following:

- **Produced a multi-ethnic visitors guide.** The 48-page booklet gives visitors an overview of four ethnic communities in King County: Native American, Asian American/Pacific Islander, African American, and Latino/Hispanic. The guide describes each community's cultural events, cultural and historic sites, arts organizations, media, religious congregations, and resource organizations.
- **Established an internship program.** S-KCCVB's paid internships enable qualified minority graduates to work at the convention center or a hotel for six months. Some students remain on the job after graduation, while some find other jobs in the tourism industry.
- **Formalized a link to the community.** The minority program director conducts outreach programs and maintains a communications link with various ethnic communities. That keeps S-KCCVB staff abreast of current events and issues.

The bureau also sponsors seminars and mini-trade shows to show-case minority business enterprises. Staff often counsel minority vendors how to do business with hotels and restaurants; at the same time, S-KCCVB sponsors forums that bring vendors together with purchasers for major corporations. The bureau's latest endeavor is to attract more minority conventions to the city.

Chapter 10

QUESTIONS AND ANSWERS

The experiences of the organizations showcased in Chapters 2 through 9 can help you assess your organization's readiness for diversity and develop an action plan. But you may still have some nagging questions: What's the right approach for my organization? Is there a compelling marketplace argument for diversity in my field? How can I overcome organizational and individual resistance?

This chapter poses and answers 18 such questions, preparing you to address salient issues before moving to Chapter 11 (Helping Your Organization Win With Diversity). Exhibit 4 lists all the questions addressed in this chapter.

What's the Role of White Men in Diversity?

Backlash against diversity has occurred in organizations that have excluded white males from significant roles in the movement—or have used misguided diversity trainers or consultants. But the fact remains that white males will constitute the bulk of the leadership roles in most organizations for some time. If these men don't participate in the movement to encourage an inclusive and productive workforce, the attempts surely will fail. In the organizations that are winning with diversity, white males contribute to the cause at all levels, from the board of directors and CEO on down.

Don't get us wrong. It's true that, without help, many white men "just don't get it"—they don't understand why an orchestrated effort is needed to change the climate and practices of American organizations. And they have good reason.

Most organizational cultures were built around value systems of middle-class, heterosexual, married, white males. They have the luxury of operating on automatic pilot with regard to the issues that frustrate others. Further, many older white men have little experience dealing with peers or subordinates who aren't just like them.

You need to employ special strategies for helping these men appreciate differences, develop new skills, and lobby for organizational change. For example, those feeling disconnected from the diversity effort can increase their comfort zones by:

- Forming professional associations with women, people of color, and people with disabilities.
- Offering to serve as mentors to people of difference.
- Subscribing to publications targeted to nonwhite males.

While in this learning mode, they should also develop their skills at team building and participatory decision making and learn to refrain from conversations that demean or denigrate others. Using these new skills, they can put their insights and experiences to work in building inclusive organizations.

In working with organizations to implement diversity initiatives, we've identified several key strategies for white males in leadership roles:

- **Define the diversity effort as the recognition and respect of differences.** Diversity means more than racial and ethnic minorities and women. The term also encompasses people with specific attributes, abilities, orientations, and characteristics as diverse as socioeconomic status, nationality, and geographic location. Under this definition, everyone in the organization must be in a learning mode.
- **Emphasize the marketplace argument for diversity.** Every organization must deal effectively with diversity among its employees and customers to succeed in the 1990s and in the next century. Every type of organization, whether for profit or nonprofit, has a marketplace

argument for diversity. Typically, white males can understand and endorse this concept.

- **Communicate the CEOs and top management's commitment to winning with diversity.** The entire organization must reflect that commitment by word and deed, individually and as a team.
- **Provide the necessary training and consultation.** Focus training on valuing diversity, understanding what it's like to be different, and building inclusive organizations. CEOs may need diversity mentors or coaches to advise them. Some use employee affinity groups—black women, single parents, physically challenged workers, or Hispanic men, for example—to advise them on how to change organizational practices that negatively affect performance.
- **Identify and eliminate barriers to high performance.** All organizational cultures are riddled with policies, practices, and expectations that impede the effective performance of different groups. Typically, these aspects of the organizational culture are unintended—but they're still oppressive and must be removed to gain employee commitment.
- **Introduce standards of behavior that affirm inclusiveness.** Evaluate, promote, and compensate employees and managers on the basis of their capacity to build inclusiveness from a diverse workforce.

References of Interest: *Beyond Race and Gender: Unleashing the Power of Your Total Work Force by Managing Diversity* (Thomas, 1991), *What Every CEO Already Knows About Managing Diversity* (Work, 1993), "White, Male, and Worried," *Business Week* (Galen and Palmer, 1994), "How to Make Diversity Pay," *Fortune* (Rice, 1994), and "Backlash: The Challenge to Diversity Training," *Training and Development* (Moseley and Payne, 1992).

How Should Meeting Professionals Confront Site-Selection Politics?

Meeting professionals find it impossible to avoid site-selection politics. At a minimum, they should be honest and literally put all the cards on the table for the client or meeting sponsor. That means addressing the sensitivities of all parties (and groups within the parties). The manner in which the planner deals with the issues relating to diversity says a great deal about his or her professionalism and skill.

For corporate or association meeting professionals, it's relatively easy to understand and reflect the sensitivity of their employing organization. Independent meeting professionals must analyze and respond with sensitivity to the different needs of many clients. But all successful meeting professionals must have the capacity to represent clients' needs and not let personal views intrude.

Site-selection politics touch on complex issues. For example, some locations appear to be inhospitable to women, racial and ethnic minorities, or gays and lesbians. Your organization may want to avoid those locations, or it may take the opposite view and favor certain cities precisely because they've been boycotted by other groups. Or perhaps your employer or client gives extra consideration to cities with a strong pro-labor orientation.

Of course, the destination isn't the only issue. The policies and reputation of a particular hotel property also come into play. You may want to review a potential site's reputation in labor matters, customer service, vendor relations, and commitment to diversity. The use of minority- or women-owned vendors also may be important.

A core competency for successful meeting professionals is the capacity to help sponsors understand the implications of location politics. Further, to help educate and guide meeting sponsors, planners need to confer with colleagues, extensively research the areas being considered, and develop contacts in these areas.

References of Interest: "Miami's Quiet Riot," *Successful Meetings* (Adams) and "Racism at Meetings," *Successful Meetings* (Conlin).

Why Are Meeting, Hospitality, and Association Groups Well-Positioned to Lead the Way on Diversity?

For starters, these industries have highly visible, well-respected organizations that represent a wide range of participants. For example, the audiences of the five organizations that sponsored this handbook include convention and visitors bureaus, corporate and association meeting professionals, exhibit managers, and executives from all types of associations. The organizations serve secondary audiences that include hotels, airlines, exhibitors, destination marketing companies, speakers bureaus, a wide range of product vendors, consultants, and volunteer leaders.

In addition to their wide reach, these organizations and their members are becoming increasingly market driven. Therefore, they can all understand the marketplace argument for diversity and its effect on their bottom line.

Third, these organizations are highly interconnected and often imitate successful practices. Once they understand how the techniques of managing diversity can lead to marketplace success, they'll eagerly apply those practices in their particular settings.

How Can We Avoid Conflict?

You can't. Make no mistake about it: Dealing with diversity can lead to conflict within your organization. But ultimately you'll experience *more* conflict if you don't make the effort.

Writing in *The Washington Post*, Dorothy Gilliam recently described the efforts of "Unity," an alliance of four organizations of minority journalists. She made the following points:

- It takes hard work to live up to the ideals of diversity—working and socializing with people from different racial and ethnic backgrounds.

- To resolve conflicts that result from diverse groups working together, members must be able to distinguish individual human barriers from cultural barriers.
- People must talk honestly from the heart and soul, exposing their values and beliefs to their colleagues.

References of Interest: "The Conquest of Hate," *Los Angeles Times Magazine* (Njer, 1993), "Righting the Wrongs of Racism," *Christian Science Monitor* (Smith, 1989), and "Morsels from the Table of Unity," *The Washington Post* (Gilliam, July 23, 1994).

Is Diversity Exclusively for Large Organizations?

Absolutely not. Indeed, the flexibility and valuing of differences that characterize inclusive organizations are achieved most easily in smaller organizational units and work teams.

Large corporations and philanthropic organizations instituted many of the early diversity programs. Their leaders had the vision to understand the significance of the demographic changes in American society and the implications of operating in a global economy. Having the CEOs of these large organizations commit to inclusiveness was critical. But the real action takes place on the front lines, where employees deal with customers, members, and clients. Although corporate philosophy provides the context, genuine buy-in occurs in branch offices, local chapters, or work units.

Smaller organizations have the advantage of being able to change more quickly. Jim Preston, CEO of Avon, has observed that fundamentally changing an organization requires one year per level. That has translated into a seven-year program for Avon. Smaller organizations with fewer levels of management can transform themselves much more rapidly.

Can an Organization in a Divided Community Value Diversity?

It's difficult for an organization to make progress within a community split by differences. Yet such communities are most in need of a common pursuit that moves people beyond old antagonisms to work together.

When United Way of America launched "Project Blueprint" to expand minority participation in local affiliates, it solicited proposals from communities that had experienced racial tensions and community divisiveness, such as West Point, Mississippi, and Pontiac, Michigan. These communities saw local initiatives to value diversity as an important component of the healing process.

In fact, organizations have a substantial advantage. Communities and society at large must deal with tremendously diverse populations. It's difficult for people with divergent values and goals to identify shared values—especially if they concentrate on past wrongs rather than current solutions. But a hotel, corporation, or association serves a specific group of customers, advances a particular cause, or supports a profession or trade. As business enterprises, these organizations have a clear market-place purpose and can establish a set of shared values. Moreover, organizations can and should remove artificial barriers to the fulfillment of those shared values. Recognizing and rewarding people for understanding and serving customer needs doesn't go unnoticed even in a divided community.

Reference of Interest: *The Spirit of Community: Rights, Responsibilities, and the Communitarian Agenda* (Etzioni, 1993).

Can People Be Persuaded To Change Their Values and Behavior?

Yes, people can change. But it's not easy. Conventional wisdom holds that one must change people's values in order to change behavior. Experience, however, shows this exercise to be both time consuming and imperfect. In fact, research shows that many of the changes in values associated with affirmative action and valuing diversity don't fully "take" during initial training; in other words, some people simply don't understand. Others keep their skepticism hidden. This reservoir of opposition impedes efforts for change.

A more effective approach involves parallel tracks. On one, continue training people and teaching them about the moral and workforce arguments for diversity. On the other track, make the marketplace argument for diversity—eliminate barriers to performance, develop performance standards that require inclusiveness-affirming behavior, and use diverse teams to solve complex issues.

These opportunities will illustrate to skeptics that the organization can win with diversity. It also shows that inclusiveness-affirming behavior and marketplace success are essential to their personal success and advancement in the organization. This realization typically changes both behavior and values. If not, the recalcitrant employee needs to find another organizational culture that better fits his or her values.

Communication helps people change. Leaders must first talk to individuals and groups to understand how the organization's rules and procedures fail to value diversity. These conversations should involve staff, members, and customers. It's also necessary to break down stereotypical ways of thinking about people. Ultimately, people should treat one another as unique individuals whose needs and characteristics must be understood. Diverse work teams quickly disabuse people of stereotypical thinking.

Reference of Interest: *Cultural Diversity in Organizations: Theory, Research & Practice* (Cox, 1994).

Do We Build Diverse Work Teams Using a Noah's Ark Approach?

Some people favor the "Noah's Ark" model for building diverse work teams—one or two members from each designated diversity group. This assumes that having people of difference on a work team designates them as the spokespeople for issues pertaining to their group. To deal with women customers, consult women on staff; to understand Asian issues, turn to the Asian expert, and so on.

Life is more complex than that. Opinions within a particular group can vary to extremes, making it impossible for one person to predict how his or her group will react to something. Furthermore, employees don't want to be "niched," nor do customers expect to be "matched" with someone like them—they expect courteous, effective service, period. Members of work teams need to be receptive to signals from diverse groups of customers. Together, they can devise approaches that meet the needs of individuals within those groups.

You simply can't assume that one person can speak for all of a group. Likewise, you can't assume that someone is sensitive to all differences just because he's a minority or she's a woman. Nor are all white males insensitive and oppressive. Organizations doing business in the 21st century can't tolerate such assumptions.

How Can We Avoid Diversity Backlash?

Two phenomena contribute to much of the backlash against diversity. One occurs when the diversity training and underlying concepts aren't sufficiently compelling to overcome the prejudices, inertia, and insecurities of people in the organization.

The second has its roots in once-popular training programs that focused on exposing racism, raising consciousness about organizational oppression, and emphasizing the transformative power of Workforce 2000's rainbow coalition. This approach tended to stereotype and isolate white males. In some cases, ineffective and poorly trained diversity consultants exacerbated the problem, further dividing and angering employees. Diversity opponents seized on media reports of backlash to promote skepticism.

Fortunately, organizations that have skillfully managed diversity have escaped these experiences. Their diversity training uses balanced, ✗ multicultural teams and takes care not to demonize white males but to identify important, constructive roles for them in the change process. Successful organizations also ground the concept of managing diversity in a long-term strategic goal, tying their efforts to success in the marketplace.

References of Interest: *The Rage of a Privileged Class* (Cose, 1993), *The Scar of Race* (Sniderman and Piazza, 1993), "Backlash! The Challenge to Diversity Training," *Training & Development* (Mobley and Payne, 1992), "The Unfortunate Side Effects of 'Diversity Training'," *New York Times* (Murray, 1993), "The Downside of Diversity," *Training & Development* (Thomas, 1994), and "White, Male, and Worried," *Business Week* (Galen and Palmer, January 31, 1994).

What's Wrong With the Traditional Organizational Culture?

Industrial-era organizational cultures did just fine when they enabled American institutions to establish preeminence in the last half of the 20th century. But that's old news.

In the words of Dennis Longstreet of Ortho Biotech, the crux of the problem is that organizational cultures were "designed by 55-year-old white males from New Jersey." These men had wives at home to raise the family; they played golf, went to church on Sunday, and had the personal support systems and financial resources to operate within an inflexible organizational culture. Because the culture was monolithic and inflexible, Mr. New Jersey didn't need to understand others. He could operate on his internal automatic pilot.

Today, none of these assumptions holds. The diversity of the workforce and the marketplace has increased, causing inflexible, monolithic organizational cultures to become dysfunctional. The traditional culture failed to accommodate changes in the marketplace and failed to win commitment from its employees. Typically, this increasing dysfunction wasn't malicious but literally unconscious. And organizations that have been slow to respond have been hammered in the marketplace.

Take Avon, for example. Originally it was a very paternalistic organization where management "took care of the ladies" who formed its sales force. Its leadership was white, male, and affluent. But these managers failed to anticipate and respond to the increase in working women in the 1970s and 1980s. As a result, Avon lost ground to competitors and missed tremendous opportunities.

The message came through loud and clear. In its latest round of cultural changes, Avon dramatically increased the diversity of its management team and introduced more organizational flexibility.

In the organizations we studied, even white males in top management understood the need to change. Once the old culture failed to make business sense, they abandoned it without remorse. But some resistance and insecurity surfaced among other white males, especially lower-level and mid-level managers over the age of 50. Typically, these men were comfortable with the old culture, unfamiliar and uncomfortable with cultural diversity, and uncertain of their capacity to change. If you don't confront the concerns and insecurities of these traditional thinkers, they can scuttle efforts to change the organization. You must show them how the traditional culture no longer makes sense.

References of Interest: *Cultural Diversity in Organizations: Theory, Research & Practice* (Cox, 1994), *The Spirit of Community: Rights, Responsibilities, and the Communitarian Agenda* (Etzioni, 1993) and "The New Post-Heroic Leadership," *Fortune* (Huey, 1994).

What Does It Mean "To Move Beyond Affirmative Action"?

When organizations say they've moved beyond affirmative action, they don't mean to suggest they've abandoned their commitment to increasing the diversity of their workforce and to measuring progress against those goals. Quite the contrary. These organizations have discovered that merely attaining numerical goals for a limited set of targeted groups wasn't enough. Many people recruited under affirmative action had failed to succeed; others who had succeeded ended up stigmatized or shepherded into narrowly defined career tracks. To tap a diverse workforce's full potential, human resource managers concluded that they needed to focus on understanding the determinants of—and barriers to—successful performance.

Some employees from targeted groups may be skeptical about broadening the concept of diversity. They will fear a dilution of influence and a retreat from the organization's commitment to affirmative action.

To win the support of these employees, confront the issue directly and honestly. First, redouble your efforts to recruit and promote diverse employees by systematically eliminating barriers to performance. This ingredient has been missing from past affirmative action efforts. To eliminate barriers and achieve employee buy-in, organizations have used a combination of affinity groups, ongoing discussions, diverse teams focusing on cultural redesign, and outside consultants.

Second, emphasize the marketplace argument for diversity, especially the importance of understanding and responding to the needs of diverse customers. In many cases, people of difference have experience in dealing with multiple cultures; they'll be happy to discover their experience is considered a core competency. Affirmative action often is associated with giving people special consideration on the basis of their race or gender. Valuing and managing diversity recognizes the capacity to work with and understand people of diverse cultures as a positive.

Reference of Interest: "The Tragic Error of Affirmative Action," *Wall Street Journal* (Kristol, 1994).

How Can Diversity Become Part of Mainstream Management?

Most organizations initially designate valuing diversity as a human resource initiative. As they develop experience with diversity and move toward inclusiveness, they see the need for all employees to internalize the concepts. Responsibility must move from the human resource department to line operations for diversity and inclusiveness to become part of the mainstream.

This shift occurs only when top management clearly states the marketplace argument for diversity and outlines the consequences of inaction. Another strategy is to link inclusiveness to other issues of personal and team effectiveness. This may involve, for example, including "winning with diversity" as a central component of training and team-building exercises for TQM and process reengineering. In selecting process reengineering and TQM teams, create diverse working groups appropriate to the task. Also emphasize the importance of performance measures related to behavior that affirms inclusiveness.

References of Interest: *Cultural Diversity in Organizations: Theory, Research & Practice* (Cox, 1994), *Workforce America! Managing Employee Diversity as a Vital Resource* (Loden, 1991), "Valuing and Managing Diversity," *Info-Line Practical Guidelines for Training and Development Professionals* (Payne and Mobley, 1993), and "Creating a Multicultural Association," *Leadership* (Bryant, 1991).

How Does Diversity Fit With Strategic Planning?

Strategic planning deals with the fundamental realignment between an organization's intent and a changing environment. Given the magnitude and importance of increasing workforce and marketplace diversity, managing diversity should become a central strategy for any high-performing organization. Everyone, from the board of directors and CEO down through all managers and employees, should understand the strategy's importance.

Most of the organizations profiled in this book have elevated managing diversity to this strategic level. They've made a clear connection between diversity and the marketplace, one that drives their decision making. On the other hand, some organizations we reviewed haven't yet achieved that plane of development. They see diversity as a value of the organization, or an important workforce initiative, but haven't fully embraced the marketplace argument.

Making the marketplace argument for diversity forms the foundation for starting or reinvigorating a diversity initiative. The CEO and the management team should use this rationale to drive the design of diversity initiatives; guide the introduction of diversity into ongoing TQM, customer service, empowerment, and team building initiatives; and shape the role of managing diversity in strategic planning.

What Does Diversity Mean to Minority-Focused Organizations?

Minority-focused organizations and institutions were founded at a time when mainstream organizations didn't value diversity. With that situation changing, some question today's role for minority-focused organizations.

But, according to John Crump, executive director of the National Bar Association (NBA), Washington, D.C., "There's more need now [for the NBA] than in 1925 when blacks couldn't join the American Bar Association (ABA)." NBA offers black lawyers opportunities to concentrate on and solve problems not likely to be addressed by the ABA, says Crump. Members can gain leadership experience more quickly and network more effectively. Additionally, the associations recognize the unique perspectives and rewards each has to offer. ABA and NBA have worked together on a number of programs, membership development, and a crime summit.

NBA membership continues to grow. "Our approach to diversity is not limited to social issues; we're always looking at what we have to do with others by necessity," says Crump. "NBA membership is a way of life, not just a professional society."

It appears that minority-focused professional societies will continue to play important and significant roles, especially since many majority institutions still have a way to go to become fully inclusive. In engineering, medicine, and other professional fields, minority organizations work in partnership with majority associations to address future workforce and recognition issues.

For example, the National Medical Association (NMA) represents African American physicians but welcomes all physicians who share its mission to reach underserved communities. NMA works with the American Medical Association (AMA) as well as with Hispanic, Asian, and Pacific groups to stay on top of the health concerns of minority communities.

Minority-owned companies and minority-focused associations have developed exceptional skills at understanding traditional, majority-focused organizational cultures. This effort hasn't been reciprocated. Organizations such as the National Minority Supplier Development Council work to redress the balance by helping majority companies understand and effectively use minority vendors. These efforts will continue to grow as minority-focused organizations represent themselves with increasing effectiveness to the traditional business community. As traditional organizations become more inclusive, however, minority-focused organizations may need to change, too.

Are We Properly Preparing Tomorrow's Workforce?

We need to do a better job of preparing students to work in environments that balance diversity and inclusiveness. They need to know how to work as members of diverse teams and how to address complex problems together.

On one hand, global society is witnessing an interesting pattern of cultural hybridization and unification. International styles in music, fashion, recreation, sports, and food are developing. Although influenced strongly by the United States, these styles incorporate elements from many countries. For example, teenagers in Manila, Chicago, Amsterdam, and Caracas listen to the same types of music, wear the same styles of clothes, and cheer the same sports stars. Distinctive foods from different countries have permeated American culture and, as more people travel internationally, they're developing more cosmopolitan tastes.

On the other hand, dramatic reactions to economic and political unification have materialized in some parts of the world. The European

Economic Union, for example, has encountered rough waters. The actions of the French to protect their film industry, language, and cuisine from the insidious assault of international (translation: American) culture seem humorous on a superficial level. Yet such actions also point to a serious issue—the tendency of a majority culture to overwhelm minority cultures.

Closer to home, many African Americans, Hispanics, and Asian Americans now choose to affirm their cultural heritages rather than assimilate into the dominant American culture. Even as that culture is changing to reflect new influences, some communities retain their language, customs, and identity. Conversely, many members of the same communities welcome assimilation—but on their terms. These different approaches create a diversity of opinion and behavior within each community. Accelerated trends toward cross-marriage have further blurred distinctions and created new definitions of diversity.

Further muddying American waters is what the media have labelled "the voluntary resegregation" of minority students on American college campuses. On one level, these actions are a response to the predominant culture on campus and that culture's inflexibility to change. Such actions also reflect the tendency of colleges to encourage exclusive groupings of people with similar interests or characteristics. Minority students create their own insulated culture not only to affirm their identity but also to take advantage of one last opportunity to seek the comfort of association before embarking on careers in multicultural or predominantly white organizations.

In any case, the university experience isn't a preparation for the real world but a retreat from it. In *Dogmatic Wisdom: How the Culture Wars Divert Education and Distract America*, Russell Jacoby puts the situation in perspective. "Even the most radical Afrocentric ideologue is culturally an American," he says. Jacoby reports on conversations with campus African American nationalists who plan to join the mainstream economy. When asked if a person could be an Afrocentrist and work for IBM, students would reply without hesitation: "Yes!"

References of Interest: *The Inclusive University: A New Environment for Higher Education* (Committee on Policy for Racial Justice, 1993), *Developing the Global Work Force* (CPC Foundation/Rand Corporation), "Diversity, Correctness, & Campus Life: A Closer Look," *Change* (Daniels, 1991), "Race on Campus," *U.S. News and World Report* (Elfin, 1993), "Academe Can Take the Lead in Binding Together the Residents of a Multicultural Society," *The Chronicle of Higher Education* (Hayes-Bautista, 1992), "Can We Talk? We'd Better or Else Multicultural America Is in Big Trouble," *The Washington Post* (Jacoby, 1994), "College Dorms Reflect Trend of Self-Segregation," *The Washington Post* (Jordan, 1994), "Frustration, Not Anger, Guides Race Relations on a College Campus," *Wall Street Journal* (Stern and Gaiter, 1994), "A Darker Shade of Brown," *The Washington Post* (Welsh, 1994), and "Equal But Separate" (60 Minutes, 1993).

How Can High-Performing Organizations Deal With Employees Who Promote Separatism?

Inclusive organizations balance a respect for differences with promotion of a multicultural environment in which no one culture predominates. An attitude of separatism fosters fragmentation and can run counter to inclusiveness.

People who hold strong views about their cultural identity or lifestyle can succeed in a high-performing, inclusive organization—but only under one condition. They must be able to behave in inclusiveness-affirming ways and operate as effective members of cross-cultural teams. That requires leaving some strongly held beliefs and even prejudices at the door. They must participate in a shared culture, values, and behaviors that have been crafted with the goal of enabling people of different cultures to work together effectively.

Holding on to sources of identity and distinctiveness—sometimes referred to as "self-affirming behavior"—doesn't necessarily promote separatism. But today's organizations must teach employees that they can't aspire to successful careers or business ventures without the capacity and willingness to deal with diverse customers, partners, employees, and colleagues. Anyone not teaching that lesson is failing to prepare their students, children, or associates for success in the 21st century.

References of Interest: *Managing in a Plural Society* (Hamzah-Sendut, Madsen, and Thong Tin Sin, 1989) and *The Spirit of Community: Rights, Responsibilities, and the Communitarian Agenda* (Etzioni, 1993).

Is the Marketplace Argument Appropriate for Nonprofit Organizations?

Yes, even nonprofits have embraced the principles of market-directed management. They define "market directed" as understanding and meeting the wants and needs of their stakeholders, members, and customers. It means going beyond a "gut feeling" to actually measure wants and needs. For nonprofits, being market driven doesn't mean that every decision is profit driven; some choose to subsidize unprofitable ventures that are central to their mission, if their members or stakeholders wish to do so.

Being market driven also doesn't mean that the organization can be cavalier about its working environment. Indeed, to succeed in today's competitive marketplace, an organization must create an empowered, flexible work environment. But empowerment without market-driven standards creates an individual-driven or staff-driven environment. Organizations adopting that model won't survive in the face of competition.

The 1990s have already provided abundant evidence that the 21st century will become the customer-driven era. This change will affect all organizations. As customers experience world-class service and performance from organizations in one sector of their lives, they will transfer those performance expectations to other organizations. Even the fields of medicine, law, and education—the last bastions of provider-driven cultures—are under increasing pressure to become service- and customer-oriented.

References of Interest: "Creating a Multicultural Association," *Leadership* (Bryant, 1991), "Managing Diversity in Nonprofits," *NSFRE Journal* (Fields, 1990), and "Diversify or Die: The New Mandate for Nonprofits," *The National Voter/The League of Women Voters* (Gray, 1993).

Can Employees Lead a Successful Diversity Initiative Without the CEO's Support?

In many settings, employees take the initiative before the CEO makes a full commitment to diversity. This is an excellent tactic for activating diversity-building efforts once the commitment has been made. But for diversity building to be recognized as a truly strategic initiative, the CEO must demonstrate enthusiasm and support.

The major barrier to CEO commitment has been a failure to communicate the marketplace argument for diversity building. Commitment usually follows an effective articulation of the link between managing diversity and establishing competitive advantage.

CHAPTER 11

HELPING YOUR ORGANIZATION WIN WITH DIVERSITY

T he principles outlined in this book can work in any setting. Their application will depend on the organization's history, characteristics, and marketplace conditions. For example, your organization may need to start from scratch and introduce new diversity programs. Or perhaps you can reshape and reconfigure existing affirmative action programs to reflect the principles of winning with diversity.

CHAMPIONS OF DIVERSITY

Whatever your organization's stage of development, the first step is clear: Understand the marketplace argument for diversity in your setting. Know how its effects will permeate all aspects and all levels of your organization. With this concept as a foundation, you'll greatly increase your chances for success.

The marketplace link is key to winning the support of line managers and employees as well. Many people see diversity as a special initiative "owned" by the human resource staff. For diversity goals to successfully permeate the organization, diversity champions in the human resource department must win converts in line management. This commitment can emerge from well-designed and managed diversity training sessions. These sessions usually prove most effective after commitment from the CEO has been achieved.

In all of our case studies, intense CEO commitment was an integral factor to an organization's success with diversity initiatives. He or she must effectively and frequently communicate how the organization will manage diversity in its pursuit of an inclusive work environment and of marketplace success. Still, many CEOs shy away from making that commitment, even in some of the organizations we profiled. This happens when they don't fully understand the marketplace argument for diversity. But if it's properly communicated, no CEO can resist the argument.

This book is specifically designed to develop a commitment to diversity based on the marketplace argument. High-level, strategic commitment facilitates the incorporation of diversity goals into every strategy, initiative, and program.

Assessing Your Organization's Readiness

While developing CEO commitment and diversity champions, you'll need to assess your organization's readiness for diversity and inclusiveness. This two-part process involves conducting a diversity/inclusiveness assessment and choosing leverage points for action.

Conducting an Assessment

To apply the market-driven model of diversity to your organization, you'll need to evaluate the status of current diversity concepts and initiatives. This assessment can be as simple as a back-of-the-envelope review by the human resource manager. Or it can be as complex as a comprehensive and sophisticated assessment. Another option: Have external consultants conduct focus groups of employees and customers at different levels. Choose the approach that matches your organization's needs and resources.

Whatever approach to assessment you choose, address the following questions:

1. What is the level of commitment to diversity?
2. Are important decisions made by diverse groups? At what levels?
3. What's the nature of current affirmative action and diversity-building programs?
4. How do you use communications and image-building activities to promote diversity?
5. Who currently receives diversity training? How is the training delivered?
6. How do you use data and information to support diversity building?
7. How do performance evaluations, promotion decisions, and compensation decisions reflect a commitment to diversity and inclusiveness-affirming behavior?
8. How are you eliminating cultural barriers to performance?
9. How extensively do you use cross-functional teams?
10. In what manner is diversity incorporated into the strategic plan?
11. Do you have organizational programs for TQM, process reengineering, customer service, empowerment, or team building? If so, is diversity a significant factor in these programs?
12. What role does diversity play in community relations and philanthropic programs?
13. Are meetings planned and designed to be accessible and useful to everyone?

(For more detailed questions you can tailor to your organization, see Exhibit 5.)

EXHIBIT 5 - ASSESSING YOUR ORGANIZATION'S READINESS FOR DIVERSITY AND INCLUSIVENESS

An Exemplary Set of Questions

1. **Level of Commitment to Diversity**
   a. How committed to diversity is your leadership team?
      –Board of Directors
      –CEO
      –Top-level management
      –Middle management
   b. How do the members communicate this commitment? Is this communication effective? Adequate?
   c. Who is "responsible" for diversity in your organization? Is "ownership" of responsibility shared throughout the organization?

2. **Decision Making**
   a. When important decisions are made by your organization, does the decision-making body or team reflect the diversity of your customers or membership? Does this vary at the following levels?
      –Board of Directors
      –Ceo and top-level management team
      –Marketing and product development
   b. When important decisions are made, do you attempt to understand the perspectives of diverse groups of customers or members? Do you conduct formal, segmented market research? How are these perspectives used by decision makers to guide their decisions?
   c. Have you suffered any examples of seriously flawed decisions—new products that failed, old services that did not appeal to a broad range of members, or opportunities that were not taken—that are attributable, partially or fully, to a lack of diversity among key decision makers? Can you answer this question?

3. **Affirmative Action and Diversity-Building Programs**
   a. What is the nature of your current affirmative action programs?
      –Workforce and labor pool monitoring
      –Recruitment
      –Monitoring of advancement and progress
   b. Have you moved beyond affirmative action to valuing diversity or managing diversity (see Appendix A)? If so, what programs have you initiated?

4. **Use of Communications and Image Building to Promote Diversity**
   a. Have you reviewed your communications to remove offensive language, unfavorable imagery, and other characteristics offensive to people of difference?
   b. How do you tailor communications and marketing materials to fit the communications preferences of diverse customers or staffs? Do you select topics and issues of interest to different groups?
   c. Do you utilize communications and image-building mechanisms to communicate your commitment to diversity? What mechanisms do you employ for this purpose?

An Exemplary Set of Questions *Continued*

5. **Diversity Training Programs**
   a. How many and what proportion of staff (members/member leaders) have participated in formal diversity planning?
   b. What was the nature of the training? Who was included in the training groups? Did you use outside trainers, facilitators, or consultants, and if so, how?
   c. Is diversity awareness a part of employee orientation? Ongoing staff development?
   d. What is the orientation of staff diversity training? Understanding racism and sexism? Valuing diversity? Contribution of diversity to effective teams and marketplace competitiveness?

6. **Use of Data and Information to Support Diversity Building**
   a. What basic measures do you utilize for affirmative action and EEO purposes?
   b. What other measures do you utilize to assess the diversity of your workforce?
   c. Have you assessed barriers to and enablers of successful performance in your organization? Did you determine how these barriers and enablers affected diverse members of your workforce?
   d. Have you linked marketplace outcomes to the diversity of your teams and organizational units?

7. **Performance Evaluation, Promotion, and Compensation**
   a. Are staff and managers evaluated on their support of diversity building? How does this affect promotion and compensation?
   b. Are staff made aware of the organization's expectations for diversity-affirming behavior? In what manner?
   c. How are individuals and teams treated in formal performance evaluations?
   d. How do you measure the success of teams or organizational units in the marketplace?

8. **Inclusion of Diversity in Your Strategic Plans**
   a. Is diversity building included in your strategic plan? How?
   b. Do other strategic initiatives reflect the impact of diversity building? How?

9. **Management Initiatives That Can Be Related to Diversity**
   a. Do you have formal or informal initiatives dealing with total quality management? Process reengineering? Customer service? Empowerment? Team building?
   b. Is diversity training or awareness in any way associated with these programs?

10. **Community Relations and Philanthropic Programs**
    a. Do you assess your organization's community relations and philanthropic programs based on their contribution to your diversity-building agenda? Are the programs assessed based on their capacity to build community and solve problems in your home communities?
    b. Do you utilize your communications to expound on your commitment to community building?

11. **Meetings**
    a. What measures do you take to assure that meetings are accessible and useful for people of difference?
    b. Do you routinely assess the satisfaction of meeting goers with your efforts? How do you reflect those findings in the design of future meetings?

Choosing Leverage Points for Action

Once you've assessed the current status of diversity and inclusiveness, identify key leverage points—places to focus diversity-building efforts. These usually include the following factors:

- **CEO Commitment to Diversity.** Through words and actions, the CEO must show support of diversity efforts throughout the organization. You won't get far without this.
- **Particular Groups.** Although you must reach all groups eventually, select a starting point. Different groups may include the board of directors, the CEO, senior management, volunteer leaders, rank-and-file members, and future employees or members.
- **Employee or Member Orientation.** Orientation programs provide the perfect opportunity to set behavioral expectations for new employees or members.
- **Diversity Training and Staff Development.** Although you can start with training as a special, stand-alone program, you will want to eventually develop a time frame for integrating it into the staff development process. Training should focus on the marketplace rationale for diversity and the importance of inclusiveness-affirming behavior.
- **Meetings.** Every organization must remove barriers to access and to effective participation in meetings. This leverage point is especially critical for multicultural and international organizations—and for meeting planning organizations that identify the staging of effective meetings as a core competency.
- **Publications, Communications, and Image Building.** On one level, organizations need to purge their publications and communications of offensive or poorly chosen language, images, and design. On a higher plane, image-building activities related to diversity can differentiate your organization in the marketplace.
- **Recognition and Awards Programs.** To acquaint staff with valuing diversity, consider cultural awareness days, multicultural festivals, and recognition of accomplishments of diverse employees.
- **Cross-Functional Teams.** Leaders of organizations founded on vertical functional hierarchies (such as marketing, product development, and manufacturing)—or those that prevent cross-functional problem solving—may not understand the contribution of inclusiveness to team performance.
- **Measurement of Progress.** Most organizations limit their evaluations of progress to numerical EEO measurements. It takes time and insight to improve the measures and their uses in decision making. Organizations already using team-based performance measures can create key performance indicators (KPIs) for measuring diversity progress and outcomes.

- **Personnel Evaluation, Promotion, and Compensation.** Changing evaluation, promotion, and compensation systems takes time and produces anxiety. Most organizations base such redesigns on substantial research and proceed incrementally with implementation.
- **Elimination of Barriers to Performance.** It's pointless to deal with this issue superficially. Eliminating barriers to performance amounts to serious surgery on an organization's culture. Most organizations cannot tackle this until they're well into the managing diversity stage of development. Consider using a consultant to guide you through this process.
- **Strategic Planning.** When the marketplace rationale for building diversity is both understood and fully supported, it must become a central factor in your strategic plan.
- **TQM, Process Reengineering, Empowerment, Team Building.** If your organization has existing initiatives related to these management concepts, reshape them to include a diversity component.
- **Product Development.** Introducing a new product or service provides an excellent opportunity to demonstrate the importance of diverse teams in winning in the marketplace.
- **Community Relations and Philanthropy.** Existing efforts can be redirected to advance an emerging agenda related to diversity. Through community outreach and activities, emphasize your organization's commitment to the "community of communities."

DEVELOPING AN ACTION PLAN

Once you've assessed readiness and selected your leverage points, you're ready to develop an action plan for building diversity. This plan will reflect the distinctive character of your organization as well as its stage of diversity development; certain skills must be mastered before you can move to the next stage. Our review suggests organizations typically take four distinct approaches:

1. Develop Highly Focused Diversity Initiatives. Some organizations—or units within large organizations—are interested in very focused diversity initiatives rather than wholesale organizational change. For example:

- A meeting planning office in a major corporation wants to enhance its capacity to plan and stage barrier-free, inclusive meetings.
- An association wants to purge its publications of topics, writings, and designs that offend readers in particular groups.
- A hotel wants to reassess its community service activities to increase opportunities for staff to participate.
- A professional society wishes to expand its role in helping attract women and minorities to the profession.

Even these targeted activities should be planned within the context of an overall program. An incremental, program-by-program approach may prevent the organization from realizing the strategic potential of diversity building. An organization in this position should appreciate the marketplace rationale for diversity and use the focused initiative as a "window" for understanding broader implications of diversity.

2. Start a Diversity Program. Many organizations are essentially starting from scratch. Even if they've had an affirmative action program and isolated diversity training and recognition programs, they need to launch a new initiative. If you're in this category, the full range of activities recommended in this chapter applies.

3. Reshape or Revitalize an Existing Diversity Program. If you're at the stage of valuing diversity, you may need to overcome backlash to affirmative action and to earlier, ineffective training. Or you may merely need a more compelling organizational imperative for diversity, one you can translate into a new wave of initiatives.

4. Take a "Managing Diversity" Program to the Next Level of Development. Organizations that are effectively managing diversity are looking for assistance to elevate their program to the next level. They typically have an adequate level of commitment and have developed some good diversity training and valuing diversity skills, but they don't yet understand how to build an inclusive, high-performing environment. Organizations in this category appreciate guidance on framing the marketplace rationale, analyzing their existing efforts, and developing an action plan to move on.

Contents of the Action Plan

While tailoring your action plan for diversity building to your organization, ensure it contains the following sections:

- **Marketplace Rationale for Diversity Building.** Spell out the marketplace rationale for diversity—this sets the tone for the entire action plan. Define what diversity means to your organization.
- **Leverage Points for Diversity Programs.** Explain how diversity will be applied to the significant leverage points you identified within your organization.
- **Schedule of Events, Assignments, Responsibilities, and Time Frames.** Provide details on all events and assignments related to diversity building. Specify who's responsible for particular diversity initiatives and actions, and outline the time frames for completion.
- **Resources.** New or reallocated resources may be necessary to launch or revive diversity programs. Once inclusiveness is mainstreamed, these resources should be part of organization budgets.
- **Measurements of Success.** Include a set of measurements for determining progress and outcomes. Make them multifaceted.

- **Appendix: Assessment of Organizational Readiness for Diversity Building and Inclusiveness.** Attach the assessment you completed so readers know what factors guided development of the plan.

Epilogue

Of course you can't do this on your own. Every person in your organization must get involved in diversity initiatives. And those initiatives must become a fundamental part of your organization's culture. This will be an important milestone on the road to achieving success in your diverse marketplace.

For any organization wishing to build an inclusive, high-performing environment, a continuing process of organizational development and transformation awaits.

So now you know what it will take to win with diversity—from you, your co-workers, and your organization. You understand the importance of winning with diversity to your organization's future competitiveness. With this knowledge, you cannot be satisfied until your organization is winning with diversity.

Appendix A
The Stages of Diversity Development

THE STAGES OF DIVERSITY DEVELOPMENT

Characteristic	Affirmative Action	Valuing Diversity	Managing Diversity	Building Inclusive, High-Performing Organizations
Diversity Goals	• Recruit from targeted underrepresented groups in the workforce. • Support and maintain their advancement.	• Understand and value the contributions of people of difference.	• Develop an understanding of managing diversity to establish competitive advantage.	• Eliminate barriers to performance based on superficial differences. Establish high standards. • Establish competitive advantage.
Leadership Commitment	• Commitment can be superficial. Hidden opposition based on personal values.	• Commitment is uneven, depending on the personal values of individuals.	• Commitment increases as the marketplace linkage becomes understood.	• Commitment is total and pervasive.
Status in the Organization	• Affirmative action is seen as a special initiative or program, driven by human resource management.	• Valuing diversity is an initiative or program with a human resource focus.	• Managing diversity is a new management perspective. Human resource management increasingly involves line management in developing the concept.	• Building inclusiveness is a fundamental value of the organization, not an initiative. • Central to organizational strategy.
Rationale	• Moral argument. • Government mandates.	• Moral argument. • Workforce argument for diversity.	• Workforce argument for diversity. • Understanding the marketplace argument for diversity.	• Marketplace and workforce arguments for diversity. • Use inclusiveness to establish competitive advantage.
Primary Tools	• Hiring goals and compliance reporting, recruiting. • Consciousness raising.	• Diversity training. • Communications, recognition days, and other celebrations of diversity.	• Diversity training integrated into everyone's professional development. • Assessing and changing the organizational culture to eliminate barriers.	• Continual cultural change. • Inclusiveness, team building, continuous quality improvement, and empowerment. • Measurement of success.

The Stages of Diversity Development

Characteristic	Affirmative Action	Valuing Diversity	Managing Diversity	Building Inclusive, High-Performing Organizations
Hiring and Composition of Staff	• Staff hired considering group representation; job requirements unchanged from pre-affirmative action.	• Develop appreciation of distinctive contributions of people of difference.	• Hiring criteria include the ability of the individual to contribute to diverse teams.	• Hiring focuses on ability of individuals to commit to shared values of the organization; to participate effectively on diverse, empowered teams; and to devote energies to serving customer needs. Artificial factors and barriers to performance removed.
Targeted Groups	• Government-specified racial minorities and women. • Focus on hiring and advancement goals for targeted groups.	• Diversity definition expanded to include physically challenged, age, sexual preference, and other characteristics. • Focus on hiring and advancement and understanding the contributions of people of difference.	• Diversity definition expanded to include many multicultural groups—any distinction identified by staff as important. • Focus shifts to changing the work environment. This opens opportunities and eliminates glass ceilings.	• Affinity groups exist for any grouping deemed important by staff as a basis for identifying barriers in the culture. • Focus on eliminating organizational barriers to high performance.
Communications and Image Building	• Eliminate offensive and poorly chosen language, images, and designs.	• Recognize accomplishments of diverse individuals. • Tailor some publications, marketing materials to particular groups. • Begin to reflect diversity and inclusiveness in mainstream publications.	• Begin to convey commitment to "managing diversity" as a distinguishing characteristic.	• Marketing of products and services effectively use diversity to establish competitive advantage. • Image building conveys the organization's commitment to inclusiveness.

THE STAGES OF DIVERSITY DEVELOPMENT

Characteristic	Affirmative Action	Valuing Diversity	Managing Diversity	Building Inclusive, High-Performing Organizations
Training	• Training focuses on moral and legal requirements for affirmative action programs and how to do affirmative action. Mostly targeted at management.	• Training focuses on exposing racism, raising consciousness, changing values, understanding how diversity is important to performance. • Training begins with management, can include most staff. • Training becomes divisive when it focuses on differences and not on facilitating inclusiveness.	• Training focuses on contribution of diversity to competitiveness and how diverse teams make more effective decisions in complex, changing environments. • Training begins with management, can include staff. • Training builds on earlier valuing diversity training. • Training is "owned" by the organization as it deals with business issues.	• Diversity is an integral component of personal effectiveness training for all staff. • Training focuses on changing behavior to empowered inclusive teamwork, then changing values. • Inclusiveness training integrated with ongoing work on team productivity tools, skills, TQM, and empowerment. • Training fully owned by the organization.
Use of Consultants	• Consultants advise on how to meet affirmative action goals.	• Consultants used in diversity training and organizational assessment. • Consultants begin to advise on organizational development.	• Consultants used less in training, more in cultural assessment and change. • Consultants provide ongoing advice on organizational development.	• Consultants used on how to win with diversity. • Ongoing advice on cultural transformation.
Rewards and Recognition	• Special recognition tied to affirmative action can stigmatize.	• Provide opportunities to recognize contributions of people of difference in public meetings, publications, other communications.	• Emphasize recognition in performance evaluation. • Incentives for diversity-affirming behavior and disincentives for lack of progress.	• Rewards and recognition totally linked to performance evaluation.

THE STAGES OF DIVERSITY DEVELOPMENT

Characteristic	Affirmative Action	Valuing Diversity	Managing Diversity	Building Inclusive, High-Performing Organizations
Performance Evaluation	• Meeting affirmative action targets not a major component of management evaluation.	• Valuing diversity seldom a major component of management evaluation.	• As organizational leadership develops an understanding of how managing diversity affects the market, it develops measures for management evaluation. • Measures focus on behavior and performance.	• Managers and staff are assessed on how their behavior and performance contribute to the organization's inclusive culture and to marketplace success. • This approach links external and internal performance.
Measurement of Organizational Progress	• Measure progress in achieving affirmative action targets for hiring and staff representation at different levels.	• Measure progress in achieving affirmative action targets and exposing staff to diversity training.	• Affirmative action measures decline in usefulness as numerical composition goals are met. Use affirmative action measures to focus on units not meeting diversity goals. • Begin to develop measures linking diversity to organizational goals and marketplace success.	• Measurement of individual performance, team performance, and unit performance links diversity to marketplace success and to the organization's bottom line.
Market Research	• Not applicable.	• Not applicable.	• Begin to tie diversity to marketplace performance. First steps in developing measures for this purpose.	• Marketplace performance and organizational culture linked. Market research used to establish the linkage and measure prospective outcomes.

THE STAGES OF DIVERSITY DEVELOPMENT

Characteristic	Affirmative Action	Valuing Diversity	Managing Diversity	Building Inclusive, High-Performing Organizations
Benchmarking	• Benchmark hiring practices against the existing labor pool, and the affirmative action program against well-developed programs at other organizations.	• Benchmark valuing diversity programs against similar programs in other organizations.	• Benchmark against managing diversity programs in other organizations and how they use diversity to establish competitive advantage.	• Benchmark against world-class performers on the basis of quality, inclusiveness, team building, and empowerment; also against market performance. • Benchmarking can link internal and external reference points.
Relationship to Strategy and Strategic Planning	• Not seen as strategic.	• Not seen as strategic.	• Begins to be seen as strategic. • Focuses on building a winning workforce.	• Using diversity to win in the marketplace central to organizational strategy.
Relationship to Other Management Initiatives: – Process Reengineering – TQM – Empowerment – Customer Service	• Not related.	• Not related.	• Begin to see linkages between managing diversity and ongoing TQM, customer service, and empowerment initiatives.	• Diversity and inclusiveness become an integrated part of TQM, empowerment, and team building, which develop the organization's people assets. • They are closely linked with TQM and process reengineering, which develops the organization's process assets.

THE STAGES OF DIVERSITY DEVELOPMENT

Characteristic	Affirmative Action	Valuing Diversity	Managing Diversity	Building Inclusive, High-Performing Organizations
Decision Making	• The organization strives to hire and promote employees from targeted groups. Most are clustered at lower levels in the organization. The patterns of decision making are largely unchanged.	• The organization develops an appreciation for contributions of diverse team members.	• The organization begins to appreciate how diverse teams yield better decisions in dealing with diverse customers. The definition of diversity is broadened to include many characteristics.	• At all levels in the organization, from the board of directors to front-line service workers, decisions are made by diverse teams. Care is taken to assure that complex issues are addressed by such teams.
Exercising Leadership	• Leadership at most levels in the organization is predominantly white males. Affirmative action efforts increase the numbers of women and minorities at entry levels first.	• Discussion of the contribution of diverse persons to leadership. • Discussion of the values of sharing leadership.	• White males begin to allow other members of diverse teams to exercise leadership. • Organization begins to understand the value of shared leadership.	• Leadership/responsibility spread throughout the organization, both through diverse teams and management structures. • Leadership exercised by wide diversity of employees. White men don't always lead.

Appendix B

Bibliography

Books, Monographs, and Surveys

Committee on Policy for Racial Justice, *The Inclusive University: A New Environment for Higher Education*, Joint Center for Political and Economic Studies Press, Washington, D.C., 1993.

Committee members claim colleges and universities need to be transformed so they can provide equal opportunities for all students. Such an environment, they say, will not only nurture an appreciation and respect for diversity but also encourage the academic community to search for and understand shared values among different cultures.

Cose, Ellis, *The Rage of a Privileged Class*, HarperCollins Publishers, Inc., New York, 1993.

Based on interviews, Cose explains why many black professionals are filled with resentment and rage. He discusses why white Americans should care and covers other topics ranging from workplace issues and crime to the alleviation of "white guilt." Despite the current "age of diversity," Cose believes, the status of black Americans rates special attention. He does not, however, count affirmative action initiatives as part of the solution.

Cox, Taylor, Jr., *Cultural Diversity in Organizations: Theory, Research & Practice*, Berrett-Koehler Publishers, San Francisco, California, 1994.

Written primarily for educators, organizational development specialists, and managers, this text features Cox's model of the effect of diversity on career outcomes and organizational effectiveness. He focuses on racial/ethnic, gender, and nationality differences in the workplace, paying special attention to how cultural differences affect creativity and innovation, problem solving, and workgroup cohesiveness and communication.

CPC Foundation/RAND Corporation, *Developing the Global Work Force*, College Placement Council, 1994.

This monograph describes the findings of a study in which leaders at major corporations and universities determined the skills needed for the global workforce. Crosscultural competence was one of the key skill sets they identified.

Etzioni, Amitai, *The Spirit of Community: Rights, Responsibilities, and the Communitarian Agenda*, Crown Publishers, New York, 1993.

The manifesto for the communitarian movement, this book calls for a reawakening of Americans' allegiance to shared values and institutions—personal relations, families, schools, and neighborhoods. Etzioni calls for balanced dualism in community affairs: rights and responsibilities, pluralism within unity, and group interests in the context of shared values.

Gardenswartz, Lee, and Anita Rowe, *Managing Diversity: A Complete Desk Reference and Planning Guide*, Business One Irwin/Pfeiffer & Company, Burr Ridge, Illinois, 1993.

The authors describe the tools and techniques for successfully marshalling the talents of a diverse workforce. The advice is practical, with worksheets, activities, and charts provided to help readers implement ideas.

Greater Washington Society of Association Executives Foundation, *Conducting International Meetings*, GWSAE Foundation, Washington, D.C., 1993.

Topics covered in this comprehensive guide include planning logistics; cultural concerns; and specific suggestions for meetings held in Europe, Canada, the Caribbean, the Pacific Rim, and Russia.

HamzahSendut, T.S.D., John Madsen, and Gregory Thong Tin Sin, *Managing in a Plural Society*, Longman Singapore Publishers Pte Ltd, Singapore, 1989.

Based on their experiences in a multiracial and Asian environment, the authors discuss culture's effect on management theory and practice. They outline ways to improve productivity in a multicultural environment (Malaysian, Chinese, and Indian) and develop multicultural managers. The international perspective offered in this text challenges commonly held beliefs of business practices.

Hughes, Robert, Culture of Complaint: *The Fraying of America*, Oxford University Press, Inc., New York, 1993.

Through a series of arguments—supported by commentary on politics, historical events, and literary works—Hughes addresses the difficulties Americans have in relating to each other and to the rest of the world. Surprisingly, given the book's cultural and political perspective, the author eschews the use of politically correct language because it, too, keeps the country divided. He proposes a "generous recognition of cultural diversity" as an antidote to the fraying of America.

Institute of Medicine, *Balancing the Scales of Opportunity: Ensuring Racial and Ethnic Diversity in the Health Professions*, National Academy Press, 1994.

This book contains the report of the Institute of Medicine's Committee on Increasing Minority Participation in the Health Professions. Suggestions include not only changes in healthcare education and training programs but also community-based actions to develop interest in minority health and science careers.

Johnson, Haynes, *Divided We Fall: Gambling With History in the Nineties*, W.W. Norton & Company, New York, 1994.

In interviews with hundreds of citizens across the country, Johnson identified jobs, crime, race, schools, services, values, and leadership as major concerns. The issues of race, class, and culture are especially poignant. Johnson's treatment of the fragmenting and polarizing effects of multiculturalism, absent complementary emphasis on shared values, is very useful.

Johnson, John H., and Lerone Bennett, Jr., *Succeeding Against the Odds*, Warner Books, New York, 1989.

Subtitled "The Inspiring Autobiography of One of America's Wealthiest Entrepreneurs," this text traces Johnson's rise from the mud fields in Mississippi, through the welfare rolls, and to a number of "firsts" in the publishing, broadcasting, and fashion industries. He predicts a promising future for America if corporations learn to think in "living color" and underscores the importance of the CEO's role.

Loden, Marilyn, and Judy B. Rosener, *Workforce America! Managing Employee Diversity as a Vital Resource*, Business One Irwin, Homewood, Illinois, 1991.

These writers believe leaders of forward-thinking organizations must move from simply accepting the concept of assimilation to actively valuing diversity. They discuss the dimensions of diversity, the dynamics and negative effects of assimilation, and issues of hiring and developing people of difference. Readers also learn how to acknowledge culture clash and establish common ground among co-workers.

Morrison, Ann M., *The New Leaders: Guidelines on Leadership Diversity in America*, Jossey-Bass, San Francisco, 1992.

Based on almost 200 interviews with managers, Morrison gleaned strategies for successfully recruiting, retaining, and developing nontraditional managers. The book offers a five-step process organizations can implement to develop a diversity plan tailored to their environments.

National Action Council for Minorities in Engineering, *Retention By Design: Achieving Excellence in Minority Engineering Education*, NACME, New York,1991.

This monograph describes the pipeline for minorities in engineering and the problems involved in producing minority graduates. It also describes NACME's program to overcome the primary factors that impede minority success—ethnic isolation, lack of peer support, lack of role models, and low faculty expectations.

National Society of Professional Engineers, *The Glass Ceiling and Women in Engineering*, Washington, D.C.

NSPE sponsored a study of how cultural and organizational barriers prevent women from advancing in the engineering field. This study exposes the sometimes intentional, but often unwitting, barriers placed in the path of women, racial and ethnic minorities, and other diverse employees.

Payne, Tamara, and Michael Mobley, "Valuing and Managing Diversity," *InfoLine: Practical Guidelines for Training and Development Professionals*, Issue No. 9305, American Society for Training and Development, Alexandria, Virginia, May 1993.

This publication starts with the business rationale for investing in diversity training and concludes with possible pitfalls. It also provides tips for undertaking, implementing, and following through on a diversity program.

Schlesinger, Arthur M., Jr., *The Disuniting of America: Reflections on a Multicultural Society*, W.W. Norton & Company, Inc., New York, 1992.

Schlesinger fears that Americans are headed toward a fragmented, segregated, and tribal society. He blames politicians and educators who succumb to the separate agendas of ethnic pressure groups. Schlesinger outlines the positive outcomes of America's focus on ethnicity. But, he maintains, ethnicity also detracts from a unifying vision of America. His decidedly historical approach helps readers appreciate the nation's diversity.

Sniderman, Paul M., and Thomas Piazza, *The Scar of Race*, The Belknap Press of Harvard University Press, Cambridge, Massachusetts, 1993.

Sniderman and Piazza explore how questions of race and public policy have become intertwined. This analysis shows that white Americans are open to argument and persuasion on many racial issues. Only by understanding this dynamic, say the authors, can the challenges of racial progress be confronted.

Society for Human Resource Management and Commerce Clearing House, SHRM/CCH Survey, Society for Human Resource Management, Alexandria, Virginia, 1993.

Results of a nationwide survey of SHRM members yielded a 12-page report on how organizations are addressing the issue of diversity.

Steele, Shelby, "The Recoloring of Campus Life: Student Racism, Academic Pluralism, and the End of a Dream," *The Content of Our Character*, St. Martin's, New York, 1990.

Steele explores the development of a politics of difference on campus.

Thomas, R. Roosevelt, *Beyond Race and Gender: Unleashing the Power of Your Total Work Force by Managing Diversity*, AMACOM, New York 1991.

This book is intended for all (not just white) managers who want to address diversity issues and gain a competitive advantage for their companies. Along with discussions of the need for diversity training, Thomas offers definitions, practical exercises, examples, and strategies to help managers appreciate the dimensions upon which employees differ.

Towers, Perrin. "Communicating With a Diverse Workforce," *Communication Management Issues*, Towers Perrin, Valhalla, New York, March 1993.

This publication discards the melting-pot metaphor in favor of "stew." It also provides guidelines for building organizational support for diversity programs and tips for ensuring success.

United Way of America, *Blueprint for Board Diversity: Volunteer Leadership Training Curriculum Models*, Vol. 1., United Way of America, Alexandria, Virginia, 1994.

The ready-to-use curriculum is designed to enhance leadership and management skills, increase knowledge of cultural diversity and crosscultural communications, and teach teambuilding and team management. It's based on Project Blueprint, a program designed to increase the number of minority volunteer leaders and policy makers in the United Way system.

_____, *Blueprint for Board Diversity: A Cultural Diversity Resource Manual to Improve Board Effectiveness*, Vol. 2, United Way of America, Alexandria, Virginia, 1994.

Through this manual, United Way helps volunteer boards improve crosscultural communications. Readers can assess a board's readiness to address issues of cultural differences and discover how to create a climate that values diversity.

West, Cornel, *Race Matters*, Beacon Press, Boston, 1993.

This collection of essays addresses race in America. West examines historical perspectives and departs from traditional black-versus-white and liberal-versus-conservative views on the causes of racism. The author's no-holds-barred approach challenges readers to condemn biases against race, class, gender, and sexual orientation.

Work, John W., *What Every CEO Already Knows About Managing Diversity*, Rainbow Books, Inc., Highland City, Florida, 1993.

Work discusses the challenges that CEOs face, as well as communication issues and moral and business imperatives. He believes that workplace patterns of exclusion must be abandoned to increase national productivity, develop new markets, and achieve global competitiveness.

Articles

Adams, Michael, "Miami's Quiet Riot," *Successful Meetings*.

Adams explores the history and effects of the "Boycott Miami" movement on the city's convention and visitors bureau.

American Association for the Advancement of Science, "Minorities '93: Trying to Change the Face of Science," *Science*, Vol. 262, November 12, 1993.

This special edition of *Science* deals with the challenges of increasing the numbers of minorities in science and engineering.

Baker, R. Jerry, and D.C. Schnebelt, "Fostering Diversity Among Members," *Association Management*, February 1994, American Society of Association Executives, Washington, D.C.

The authors describe the diversity efforts of the National Association of Purchasing Management.

Bernstein, Aaron, "Inequality: How the Gap Between Rich and Poor Hurts the Economy," *Business Week*, August 15, 1994.

This article explores the effects of growing inequalities in income, education, and lifestyle between the richest and poorest segments of society.

Boot, Max, "Oppression Studies Go Corporate," *Wall Street Journal*, August 24, 1994.

This article describes new directions in diversity training, including taking a less confrontational view of diversity and moving away from stereotypes of all kinds.

Broadwell, Laura, "Valuing Diversity And Coping With The Challenges," *Association Meetings*, June 1993.

Broadwell cites statistics that show the discrepancies in representation of women and people of color in association ranks.

Bryant, Anne L., "Creating a Multicultural Association," *Leadership*, 1991, American Society of Association Executives, Washington, D.C.

The author discusses prerequisites to undertaking a diversity program and offers eight steps for creating a multicultural association.

Business Reports, "The Quiet Integration of Suburbia," *American Demographics*, August 1994.

This article highlights the growing integration of America's fastest growing metropolitan areas—and points out that high levels of segregation persist in slow-growing places.

Butler, Charles, "A Fair Way," *Successful Meetings*, May 1993.

Butler discusses the challenges of planning golf outings that accommodate the needs of the disabled players.

Conlin, Joseph, "Racism at Meetings," *Successful Meetings*.

Conlin outlines tips for fighting racism at meetings and for making life "intolerable for the bigot."

Cortés, Carlos E., "Pluribus & Unum: The Quest for Community Amid Diversity," *Change*, September/October 1991.

Citing a colleague's description of multiculturalism as "a wonderful opportunity to bring some excellent new scholarship to all levels of education," Cortés discusses competing philosophies and the implications of diversity on the college campus.

Daniels, Lee A., "Diversity, Correctness, & Campus Life: A Closer Look," *Change*, September/October 1991.

In describing America's obsession with political correctness, Daniels reports the views of academics.

Dickson, Reginald D., "The Business of Equal Opportunity," *Harvard Business Review*, January/February 1992.

Dickson describes the founding and operating philosophies of Inroads, Inc., a company that trains, develops, and places high school seniors in business and technological careers.

Eiben, Therese, "When Will Women Get to the Top?," *Fortune*, September 21, 1992.

According to Eiben, a poll of chief executive officers of America's largest companies reveals precious few of them believe women could succeed them within the next decade.

Elfin, Mel, and Sarah Burke, "Race on Campus," *U.S. News and World Report*, April 19, 1993.

The authors note that campuses nationwide have witnessed a new segregation perpetuated by choice.

Ellis, James E., "Corporate Women," *Business Week*, June 8, 1992.

According to Ellis, corporate officers have heard about the demographic changes facing America but haven't experienced them.

Fields, William I., "Managing Diversity in Nonprofits." *NSFRE Journal*, Winter 1990, National Society of Fund Raising Executives, Alexandria, Virginia.

Fields discusses the consequences of excluding nonwhites from first-team positions in philanthropy and addresses common myths that inhibit diversification.

Freeman-Evans, Tia, "The Enriched Association: Benefiting From Multiculturalism," *Association Management*, February 1994, American Society of Association Executives, Washington, D.C.

In addition to discussing barriers to diversity, Freeman-Evans outlines the rationale and requirements for attending to diversity issues.

Galen, Michele, and Ann Therese Palmer, "White, Male, and Worried," *Business Week*, January 31, 1994.

The authors offer tips for preventing "white male backlash." The article also includes statistics and projections of minorities in management.

Gilliam, Dorothy, "Morsels From the Table of Unity," *The Washington Post*, July 23, 1994.

The author reports on the unity-building efforts of four national associations that represent journalists of color—African American, Asian American, Latino, and Native American.

Gray, Sandra Trice, "Diversify or Die: The New Mandate for Nonprofits," *The National Voter/The League of Women Voters*, June/July 1993.

In addition to outlining eight steps to achieving diversity and nine obstacles to diversity, Gray emphasizes the nonprofit sector's participation.

Hayes-Bautista, David E., "Academe Can Take the Lead in Binding Together the Residents of a Multicultural Society," *The Chronicle of Higher Education*, October 25, 1992.

Hayes-Bautista protests that minorities are really the majority and that the term is no longer accurate. He believes universities should prepare students to accept and value differences rather than focus on minorities as marginal peoples.

Huey, John, "The New Post-Heroic Leadership," *Fortune*, February 21, 1994.

Many organizations are implementing the principles of continuous quality improvement, empowerment, and team building to be competitive in the global economy. In doing so, they are discovering that they must change their fundamental concepts of leadership.

Jacoby, Russell, "Can We Talk? We'd Better or Else Multicultural America Is in Big Trouble," *The Washington Post*, July 27, 1994.

Jacoby calls for Americans to discuss the issues of identity, diversity, shared values, immigration, and the national interest.

_____, "The Most Radical Afrocentric Ideologue Is Culturally an American," *The Chronicle of Higher Education*, March 30, 1994.

In this excerpt from the book *Dogmatic Wisdom: How the Culture Wars Divert Education and Distract America*, Jacoby asks if African American and Latino cultures differ significantly from the dominant American culture.

Jordan, Mary, "College Dorms Reflect Trend of Self-Segregation," *The Washington Post*, March 6, 1994.

Students are demanding dormitories defined by race, ethnicity, sexual orientation, and other categories. Citing experiences at Brown University and the University of Pennsylvania, the author elicits views from both proponents and opponents of self-segregation.

Kaplan, Robert D., "The Coming Anarchy," *Atlantic Monthly*, February 1994.

This article gives a chilling account of how scarcity, crime, overpopulation, tribalism, and disease are rapidly destroying the social fabric in many areas.

Katz, Judith, and Frederick A. Miller, "Between Monoculturalism and Multiculturalism: Traps Awaiting the Organization," *OD Practitioner*, September 1988.

This article describes 14 traps to avoid in organizations that aspire to move from monoculturalism to multiculturalism.

Kotkin, Joel, "The Entitlement Trap: Why Pushing Group Rights Is a Danger to Diversity," *The Washington Post*, February 7, 1993.

Kotkin is concerned about the pressures exerted on government by cultural and ethnic lobbies. He believes political activists and elite universities support a government role to protect the "special" needs of various groups. However, he says, most members of minority groups do not.

Kristol, Irving, "The Tragic Error of Affirmative Action," *Wall Street Journal*, August 1, 1994.

Kristol takes the view that administrative decisions and judicial action have imported affirmative action quotas into American life. This, he says, has given racial consciousness a new lease on life.

Leo, John, "A University's Sad Decline," *U.S. News and World Report*, August 15, 1994.

This article describes the decline of New York's city university system (CUNY), which replaced its standard curriculum with a nonjudgmental pedagogy.

Levine, Arthur, "Editorial: The Meaning of Diversity," *Change*, September/October 1991.

Citing study results and variations in how campuses address diversity, Levine calls on all colleges to clearly define diversity and develop long-term comprehensive plans.

Lucas, Jay H., and Mark G. Kaplan, "Unlocking the Corporate Closet," *Training & Development*, January 1994, American Society for Training and Development, Alexandria, Virginia.

The authors suggest that human resource practitioners deal with employees' sexual orientation as part of ongoing diversity efforts.

McLaughlin, Judith Block, "James O. Freedman on Diversity & Dartmouth," *Change*, September/October 1991.

In this interview, Dartmouth College's president tells why diversity must be one of the highest emphases of America's colleges. He characterizes the commitment to diversity as a long-term effort, definitely not for the faint-hearted.

Mitchell, Russell, and Michael Oneal, "Managing By Values: Is Levi Strauss' Approach Visionary or Flaky?," *Business Week*, August 1, 1994.

This article explores how Robert Haas, CEO of Levi Strauss, has introduced values of empowerment and inclusion to the entire workforce, from the top levels of management to the factory floor.

Mobley, Michael, and Tamara Payne, "Backlash! The Challenge to Diversity Training," *Training & Development*, December 1992, American Society for Training and Development, Alexandria, Virginia.

The authors describe how poor training programs can cause backlash—and how to avoid it.

Murray, Kathleen, "The Unfortunate Side Effects of 'Diversity Training'," *The New York Times*, August 1, 1993.

Murray illustrates the potential pitfalls of diversity workshops, using real-life examples where good intentions resulted in a lawsuit and increased infighting among employees.

Njer, Itabari, "The Conquest of Hate," *Los Angeles Times Magazine*, April 25, 1993.

Set in the context of the 1993 Los Angeles riot, the article describes a three-day workshop sponsored by the National Coalition Building Institute. Njer includes participants' experiences and reactions, as well as examples of how they applied the training.

O'Reilly, Brian, "The New Deal: What Companies and Employees Owe One Another," *Fortune*, June 13, 1994.

This series of articles defines the changing roles of employer and employee in the flexible, networked, teamoriented, and fragmented work environment of the 1990s.

Rice, Faye, "How to Make Diversity Pay," *Fortune*, August 8, 1994.

Many companies have found that diverse work teams and diverse management enable them to enhance productivity and establish competitive advantage. The article describes how managers have learned how to make diversity pay.

Sander, Gabrielle, "The Other Americans," *American Demographics*, June 1994.

An increasingly diverse America no longer fits into the government's four racial categories. In the 1990 Census, reports Sander, almost 10 million people created a giant statistical headache by refusing to describe themselves as white, black, Asian, or American Indian.

Seib, Gerald F., "A Black Thing: Quiet Discontent Over the System," *Wall Street Journal*, May 19, 1994.

A recent survey by Michael Dawson of the University of Chicago and Ronald Brown of Wayne State University portrays a more radical black America than existed five years ago.

Smith, David Christian, "Righting the Wrongs of Racism," *Christian Science Monitor*, October 23, 1989.

Cherie Brown, founder and executive director of the National Coalition Building Institute, discusses methods for eliminating prejudice and discrimination.

Stern, Gabriella, and Dorothy J. Gaiter, "Frustration, Not Anger, Guides Race Relations on a College Campus," *Wall Street Journal*, April 22, 1994.

The resegregation occurring on many college campuses is the result of blacks turning inward out of frustration, not animosity, say Stern and Gaiter.

Thiederman, Sondra, "Staff Diversity: The Best of All Backgrounds," *Association Management*, February 1994, American Society of Association Executives, Washington, D.C.

Thiederman applies corporate experience with diversity to the association world. She suggests steps executives can take to recruit and retain a diverse staff.

Thomas, Victor C., "The Downside of Diversity," *Training & Development*, January 1994, American Society for Training and Development, Alexandria, Virginia.

If done improperly, diversity training can cause confusion, disorder, and hostility. Thomas warns of problems stemming from the differences in the ways in which men and women communicate and from the reluctance of middle managers to speak up around their peers.

Welsh, Patrick, "A Darker Shade of Brown," *The Washington Post*, May 15, 1994.

Forty years after the U.S. Supreme Court's desegregation decision, the culture of America's colleges is more separate than ever. Welsh looks at the reasons.

Williams, Mary V., "Will Diversity = Equality for Multicultural Communicators?," *Communication World*, February 1991, International Association of Business Communicators, San Francisco.

Williams lists coping and career development strategies for multicultural communicators.

Videos

60 Minutes, "Equal But Separate," CBS, September 5, 1993. [To order call (800) 843–0048.]

This segment addresses the decision of some black students at Duke University to stake out separate territory. Feelings of both white and black students are shared as are their opinions on affirmative action, cultural differences, and the need for group identity. Although not fully developed, many other issues regarding stereotyping and racism are debated.

Appendix C

Participants in This Project

This book could not have been written without the assistance of members of the Unity Team, Task Force, and the individuals who provided profiles of their organizations. The authors of this book are grateful to the Unity Team for sponsoring the "Building Inclusive Organizations" project; the Task Force for providing ideas, guidance, and feedback; and the individuals who participated in onsite and telephone interviews for sharing their stories and demonstrating a variety of diversity projects in action.

Unity Team Members

ASAE:

Garis F. Distelhorst, CAE
  Chief Staff Executive
  National Association of College Stores
  Oberlin, OH

Staff Contact:
Ann C. Kenworthy, CAE
  Executive Director
  ASAE Foundation
  Washington, DC

IACVB:

Marrian Holt
  President
  San Jose Convention and Visitors Bureau
  San Jose, CA

Staff Contact:
Stephen C. Carey, PhD, CAE
  President Designate
  International Association of Convention
  and Visitor Bureaus
  Chevy Chase, MD

IAEM:

Karen Howe, CEM
  Vice President, Corporate
  National Trade Productions
  Alexandria, VA

Staff Contacts:
Steven Hacker, CAE
  President
  International Association for Exposition
  Management
  Indianapolis, IN

Dana Murphy
  Executive Director
  IAEM Foundation
  Indianapolis, IN

MPI:

John L. Fuller, Jr.
  Sheraton Harbor Island Hotel
  San Diego, CA

Staff Contacts:
Edwin L. Griffin, Jr., CAE
  Executive Vice President, CEO
  Meeting Professionals International
  Dallas, TX

Peter Turner
  Senior Vice President
  Meeting Professionals International
  Dallas, TX

PCMA:

David R. Evans
  Vice President
  Westin Hotels & Resorts
  Seattle, WA

Staff Contacts:
Roy B. Evans, Jr., CAE
  Executive Vice President
  Professional Convention Management
  Association
  Birmingham, AL

David DuBois
  Vice President of Marketing
  Professional Convention Management
  Association
  Birmingham, AL

Task Force Members

J. D. Andrews
  Chief Operations Officer
  National Association for the Education of
  Young Children
  Washington, DC

Ignacio A. Cabrera, CEM
  Assistant Vice President
  Exposition Sales
  National Association of Home Builders
  Washington, DC

Bonnie Cunningham
  Meeting Management Group
  Ashland, MA

Joan L. Eisenstodt
  President
  Eisenstodt Associates
  Washington, DC

Marian Holt
  President
  San Jose Convention and Visitors Bureau
  San Jose, CA

Terri L. Lawrence
  Manager, Resource Center
  Meeting Professionals International
  Dallas, TX

Vivienne Lee
  Vice President
  Resources Development Council for the
  Advancement and Support of Education
  (CASE)
  Washington, DC

Helen Cauthen Mitchell, CMP
  President
  The Meeting Advisor, Inc.
  Atlanta, GA

H. Bryan Montgomery
  Chairman
  Andy-Montgomery, Ltd.
  London, England

Spurgeon Richardson
  President
  Atlanta Convention and Visitors Bureau
  Atlanta, GA

Langley A. Spurlock, PhD, CAE
  Director
  CHEMSTAR Division
  Chemical Manufacturers Association
  Washington, DC

Lydia Succi
  Vice President
  External Human Resources and Diversity
  Division
  United Way of America
  Alexandria, VA

Melvin Tennant, II
  President and CEO
  Charlotte Convention and Visitors
  Bureau
  Charlotte, NC

Persons Interviewed/ Organizations Profiled

Dudley Powell
  Vice President
  Human Resources Administration &
  Diversity
  Allstate Insurance Company
  Northbrook, IL

Karleen Zuzich
  Diversity Director
  Allstate Insurance Company
  Northbrook, IL

William J. Myers, CMP, CAE
  Vice President & Convention Manager
  American Academy of Family Physicians
  Kansas City, MO

Anne L. Bryant
  Executive Director
  American Association of University
  Women
  Washington, DC

Jerry Peterson
  American Bankers Association
  Washington, DC

Melissa Thompson
  Staff Manager
  American Hotel & Motel Association
  Washington, DC

Austin Brown
  Director of Human Resources
  American Lung Association/American
  Thoracic Society
  New York, NY

Johnette Meadows
  Director
  Department of Minority/International
  Affairs
  American Physical Therapy Association
  Alexandria, VA

Debra Sher
  Vice President Member Services Division
  American Society of Association
  Executives
  Washington, DC

Janet McNichol
  Director of Human Resources
  American Speech Language Hearing
  Association
  Rockville, MD

Penny L. Prue
  Assistant Vice President of Human
  Resources
  Association of American Railroads
  Washington, DC

Jim Daniels
  Manager of Public Affairs
  Avon Products, Inc.
  New York, NY

Al Smith
  Director of Managing Diversity
  Avon Products, Inc.
  New York, NY

Jorge E. Castex, President
  Congress Internacionales, S.A.
  1091 Buenos Aires
  Argentina

Suvi Saxen
  Managing Director
  Congress Management Systems - Helsinki
  Helsinki, Finland

Robert Hume
  Office of Minority Educational
  Development
  Georgia Institute of Technology
  Atlanta, GA

Leslie Saunders
  Director of the Pluralism Strategy Unit
  Girl Scouts of the U.S.A.
  New York, NY

Al Church
  Regional Director of Human Resources
  for Eastern Regions
  Hilton Hotels Corporation, Eastern
  Region
  Atlanta, GA

Elizabeth Allan
  Senior Vice President
  International Association of Business
  Communicators
  San Francisco, CA

Sylindria Bynoe
  Government Relations Representative
  International Association of Fire Chiefs
  Fairfax, VA

Russell L. Abolt
  Executive Vice President
  International Sleep Products Association
  Alexandria, VA

Walter Johnson
  President and CEO
  Institute for Diversity and Health
  Management
  Atlanta, GA

Alva Wheatley
  Vice President and Manager of the
  Cultural Diversity Project
  Kaiser Permanente Health Care Program
  Oakland, CA

Sue Thompson
  Director of Human Resource
  Development
  Levi Strauss & Company
  San Francisco, CA

Ken Abrams
  Vice President Personnel
  Loews Hotel
  New York, NY

Sandy Leandro
  Diversity Coordinator
  Marriott International
  Bethesda, MD

National Action Council for Minorities in
  Engineering, Inc.

Dwight Ellis
  Vice President Human Resource
  Development
  National Association of Broadcasters
  Washington, DC

Dawn Harris
  Director of Personnel
  National Association of Home Builders
  Washington, DC

R. Jeffrey Baker
  Executive Vice President
  National Association of Purchasing
  Management
  Tempe, AZ

Luisa Lopez
  Special Assistant for Affirmative Action
  and Affirmative Action Officer
  National Association of Social Workers
  Washington, DC

John Crump, CMP
  Executive Director
  National Bar Association
  Washington, DC

Maureen Robinson
  Director of Education
  National Center for Nonprofit Boards
  Washington, DC

Wilbur V. Luna
  Manager, Human and Civil Rights
  National Education Association
  Washington, DC

Rosemary A. Davis
  Executive Vice President
  National Medical Association
  Washington, DC

Donald G. Weinert, P.E.
  Executive Director
  National Society of Professional
  Engineers
  Alexandria, VA

Sarah Colamarino
  Director for Professional Services
  Ortho Biotech
  Raritan, NJ

Andrea Zintz
  Vice President Human Resources
  Ortho Biotech
  Raritan, NJ

Thomas D. Muldoon
  President
  Philadelphia Convention & Visitors
  Bureau
  Philadelphia, PA

Steven C. Morris
  President
  Seattle-King County Convention &
  Visitors Bureau
  Seattle, WA

Jesse Stewart, Jr.
  Director of Human Resources
  Sheraton Washington
  Washington, DC

Stephen Tan
  Managing Director
  Singapore Exhibition Services PTE Ltd.
  Singapore

Grace Prindle
  Manager International Programs
  Society for Human Resource
  Management
  Alexandria, VA

John Libby
  Senior Associate, Editorial Review
  United Way of America
  Alexandria, VA

Mary Williams Stover
  Director of Diversity
  United Way of America
  Alexandria, VA

Bill Mills
  Vice President
  External Human Resources, Diversity
  United Way of America
  Alexandria, VA

Sandra Newton-Hinton
  Community Resources Manager
  United Way of King County
  Seattle, WA

Doreen Cato
  Original Staff Director
  Project Lead
  United Way of King County
  Seattle, WA

Brooke Mahoney
  Executive Director
  Volunteer Consulting Group
  New York, NY

William H. Edwards
  General Manager
  Washington Hilton and Towers
  Washington DC

James Seay
  Director of Human Resources & Diversity
  Administrator
  The Westin Crown Center
  Kansas City, MO

Eileen Erwin
  Human Resources Staff
  The Westin Hotel, Seattle
  Seattle, WA

Michael Fischer
  Human Resources Manager
  The Westin Hotel, Seattle
  Seattle, WA

George Smith
  Director, Human Resources
  The Westin Hotel, Seattle
  Seattle, WA

Johanna Howell
  Corporate Director for Staffing and
  Development
  Westin Hotels and Resorts
  Seattle, WA

Brenda Hooper
  International Conference Manager
  ZENECA Pharmaceutical
  United Kingdom

Organizations Profiled

Hospitality Industry:

American Hotel & Motel Association
Hilton Hotel Corporation, Eastern Region
Loews Hotel
Marriott International
Philadelphia Convention and Visitors
  Bureau
Seattle-King County Convention and
  Visitors Bureau
Sheraton Washington
Washington Hilton and Towers
The Westin Crown Center, Kansas City
Westin Hotels and Resorts
The Westin Hotel Seattle

International Meeting Professionals:

Congress Management Systems - Helsinki
Congress Internacionales - South America
Singapore Exhibition Services Pte Ltd.

Association Meeting Professionals:

American Academy of Family Physicians
National Association of Broadcasters
National Education Association

Corporate Meeting Professionals:

ZENECA Pharmaceuticals - England
Avon - USA
Allstate Insurance - USA
Ortho Biotech - USA

Other Corporations:

Avon
Allstate Insurance
Kaiser Permanente
Levi Strauss
Ortho Biotech
Wal-Mart

Associations:

Federations:
American Society of Association
  Executives
National Association of Purchasing
  Managers

Philanthropic:
Girl Scouts of the USA
National Center for Nonprofit Boards
United Way of America System
United Way of King County
Volunteer Consulting Group

Professional:
American Association of University Women
American Lung Association/American
  Thoracic Society
American Physical Therapy Association
American Speech Language Hearing
  Association
National Action Council for Minorities in
  Engineering, Inc.
National Association for Education of
  Young Children
National Association of Social Workers
National Bar Association
National Medical Association
National Society of Professional Engineers
Society for Human Resources Management

Trade:
American Bankers Association
American Hospital Association
Association of American Railroads
International Association of Business
  Communicators
International Association of Fire Chiefs
International Sleep Products Association
National Association of College Stores
National Association of Home Builders
National Minority Supplier Development
  Council

Universities:

California State University - Los Angeles
Georgia Institute of Technology

CHARACTERISTICS OF PARTICIPANT ORGANIZATIONS

NAME OF ORGANIZATION	TYPE OF ORGANIZATION	SIZE OF MEMBERSHIP/ CUSTOMERSHIP	ANNUAL BUDGET OR REVENUES	SCOPE OF ORGANIZATION	STAFF SIZE
Allstate Insurance Company	Corporation		$20 billion	International	50,000
American Academy of Family Physicians	Professional Association	79,000	$45 million	National	260
American Association of University Women	Professional Association	135,000	$12 million	National	90
American Bankers Association	Trade Association	10,000	>$10 million	National	400
American Hospital Association	Trade Association	5,000	>$10 million	National	825
American Hotel & Motel Association	Trade Association	12,000	$8 million	National	60
American Lung Association/American Thoracic Society	Professional Association	5,000	—	National	—
American Physical Therapy Association	Professional Association	63,000	$23 million	National	140+
American Society of Association Executives	Federation Association	22,000	$17 million	International	125
American Speech Language Hearing Association	Professional Association	73,000	$16 million	National	170
Association of American Railroads	Trade Association	75	$100 million	National	750
Avon Products, Inc.	Corporation	2.5 million	$3.8 billion	Global	30,000
California State University-L.A.	University	20,000 students	—	Comprehensive Univ.	—
Congress Internacionales S.A.	Independent Meeting Planner	15 meetings per year	$3 million	Global	12
Congress Management Systems	Professional Congress Organizer	—	—	Global	7
Georgia Tech	University	12,000 students	—	Research University	—
Girl Scouts of the U.S.A.	Philanthropic Association	3 million	$30 million	National	500
Hilton Hotel Corporation, Eastern Region	M/H Industry	15 properties	—	Regional	—
International Association of Business Communicators	Professional Association	12,000	$3.5 million	International	31
International Association of Fire Chiefs	Professional Association	10,000	$3.1 million	International	25
International Sleep Products Association	Trade Association	600	$3 million	International	17
Kaiser Permanente Health Care Corporation	Health Care	6.6 million	$11.9 billion	National	83,000

Name of Organization	Type of Organization	Size of Membership/ Customership	Annual Budget or Revenues	Scope of Organization	Staff Size
Levi Strauss & Company	Corporation	25,000	$5.6 billion	Global	32,000
Loews Hotel	M/H Industry	14 properties	—	National	—
Marriott International	M/H Industry	850 lodging properties	$9 billion	Global	154,000
National Action Council for Minorities in Engineering, Inc	Corporation	—	$2.5 million	National	20
National Association of Broadcasters	Professional Association	7,500	$20 million	National	150
National Association of College Stores	Trade Association	4,200	$8 million	National	70
National Association for the Education of Young Children	Professional Association				
National Association of Home Builders	Trade Association	170,000	$38 million	National	300
National Association of Purchasing Managers	Federation Association	36,000	$9.6 million	National	50
National Association of Social Workers	Professional Association	145,000	> $10 million	National	126
National Bar Association	Professional Association	16,000	$1.6 million	National & International	12
National Center for Nonprofit Boards	Philanthropic Association	6,000	$1.8 million	National	17
National Education Association	Professional Association	2.2 million	$178-$180 million	National	5,050
National Medical Association	Professional Association	17,000	$2-5 million	National	27
National Minority Supplier Development Council	Nonprofit Corporation	3,500 corporate mem.	—	National	42 regional offices
National Society of Professional Engineers	Professional Association	76,800	$5-10 million	National	80
Ortho Biotech, Inc.	Corporation				
Philadelphia Convention and Visitors Bureau	M/H Industry	915	$6.2 million	Philadelphia	61
Seattle King County Convention and Visitors Bureau	M/H Industry	1,050	$5.2 million	Regional	45
Sheraton Washington	M/H Industry	500,000	$66 million	Washington, D.C.	900
Singapore Exhibition Services Pte Ltd	Exhibition Services Corporation	—	—	Global	42
Society for Human Resource Management	Professional Association	60,000	$20 million	International	90
United Way of America System	Philanthropic Association	1,200	$21.3 million	National	192

INDEX